MOVING TIME

A COMPLETE GUIDE
TO GETTING READY
PACKING UP
SAYING GOODBYE
SETTLING IN
MEETING NEW PEOPLE
MAKING
NEW FRIENDS
AND FEELING
AT HOME AGAIN

MOVING TIME

BY CAROLYN TRAGER

DRAWINGS BY TOM HUFFMAN

GRAPHICS BY NICK KRENITSKY

FRANKLIN WATTS
NEW YORK | LONDON | 1978

Library of Congress Cataloging in Publication Data

Trager, Carolyn.
Moving time.

Bibliography: p.
Includes index.

SUMMARY: Offers suggestions for dealing with the practical and emotional problems inherent in moving.

1. Moving, Household—Juvenile literature. [1. Moving, Household] I. Krenitsky, Nicholas. II. Title.

TX307.T7 643 78–7722

ISBN 0–531–02219–6

Printed in the United States of America
6 5 4 3 2 1

TO ALAN

CONTENTS

MOVING TIME

THE BIG CHANGE
GLASS
1

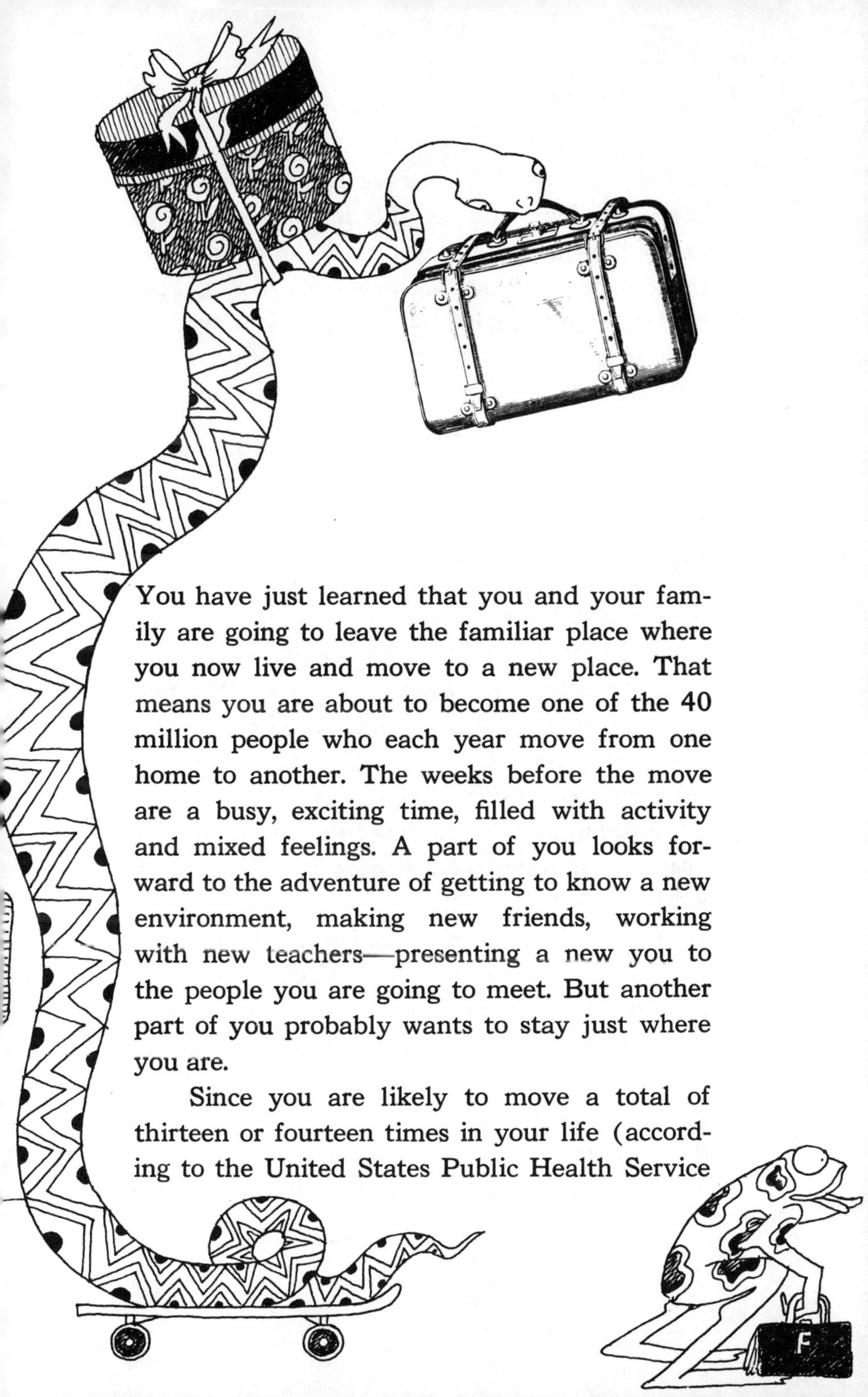

You have just learned that you and your family are going to leave the familiar place where you now live and move to a new place. That means you are about to become one of the 40 million people who each year move from one home to another. The weeks before the move are a busy, exciting time, filled with activity and mixed feelings. A part of you looks forward to the adventure of getting to know a new environment, making new friends, working with new teachers—presenting a new you to the people you are going to meet. But another part of you probably wants to stay just where you are.

Since you are likely to move a total of thirteen or fourteen times in your life (according to the United States Public Health Service statistics), one of these days you will be an expert at it. But whether this is your first move or your fifth, now is the time to start enjoying the fun and solving the problems of changing homes. A few months from now you will be looking back nostalgically on this as one of the milestones of your life, so keep cool and take things one step at a time.

HOW DO YOU FEEL ABOUT IT?

You may not have been asked whether or not you want to move, but this doesn't mean that your parents don't care about your feelings. Their decision may have been based on reasons that have more to do with practical matters than with emotions. Perhaps the family needs more room, or a house that costs less money to heat, or an apartment closer to where your mother or father works.

If you absolutely hate the thought of moving, you are not alone. Almost everybody finds it hard to take. For example, Andrew had just celebrated his tenth birthday when he moved recently for the second time. He scarcely remembered the first time because he was only three years old then, and he really didn't care where he lived as long as he had his favorite toys, his books, his television set, and his parents with him. But after living in one place for seven years he was not eager to move from the rambling house he knew so well and leave behind friends, favorite teachers, and familiar places. Andrew is an only child so he didn't have sisters or brothers to share those feelings with, but he did talk to his mother and father about them. What he discovered was that grownups get anxious about making changes too. His parents had mixed feelings about the move. They dreaded all the chores connected with moving, and they knew they were going to miss the neighbors who had become their close friends; but they felt that the advantages of a more compact house and much better office space for the law practice they shared outweighed the disadvantages. Talking these things over did not make Andrew any more enthusiastic about the move, but it did make him feel better to know that his mother and father not only understood but shared his reluctance.

WHAT TO DO ABOUT FEELING ANXIOUS

The first thing to remember is that it is perfectly normal to feel uneasy about making a major change. Almost everyone will understand your feelings and sympathize with them. Don't be embarrassed to tell your family and friends about your misgivings. Sharing those feelings, hearing yourself describe them out loud, helps put them in perspective.

A lot of the anxiety connected with change is fear of the unknown. Well, one simple way to deal with that problem is to ask questions. Your parents are not going to know what your fears are unless you tell them, and they won't know what details you are interested in unless you ask them. So try to set up a question and answer session with your parents as soon as possible. Here are some of the questions you may want answered:

- ☐ Why are we moving?
- ☐ Where is the new place?
- ☐ Is it nice?
- ☐ When are we moving?
- ☐ Can I stay at the same school, at least until the end of the term?
- ☐ Is the new place bigger or smaller than where we live now?
- ☐ Will I have my own room?
- ☐ Will I be able to walk or bicycle to school? Will I have to take a bus or subway?
- ☐ Can my friends here come to visit?

Perhaps the first person to quiz is yourself. How about asking yourself why you feel uncertain or negative about the move; don't answer with vague general reasons but with specific ones.

ON THE MINUS SIDE

Andrew made the following antimove list:

- ☐ I don't know anyone in the new neighborhood.
- ☐ The new school doesn't have a tennis court so I won't be able to practice as much once we move.
- ☐ I won't be able to see my best friends except on weekends.
- ☐ There's no good place to skateboard near the new house.
- ☐ The new house is smaller so there probably won't be enough room for all my stuff.

Does your list include some of the same sort of gripes that Andrew had? Moving into an unfamiliar apartment or house may scare you; being the new kid in class and on the block may make you feel lonely; learning where everything is in another neighborhood, and getting to know a lot of strangers, may seem like an impossible task. Packing and unpacking probably strikes you as the bore of all time. And it hurts to move away from dear friends. These are all reasonable, normal reactions to relocating, but they are not the only reactions possible. They can, and probably do, go hand in hand with a lot of other, more positive, feelings.

THE PLUS FACTORS

Having a new room is exciting. If you're like many boys and girls, you ran out of closet, shelf, and play space in the old room ages ago. You get used to familiar clutter, even if you don't like it, and it is hard to decide what to throw away or rearrange when there is no pressing need to do so. Well, the need is here now. This is your chance to create a brand new personal living space, one that fits who you are now rather than the child you were several years ago.

You will soon have a bunch of new friends. All those strangers in the new neighborhood and school will become acquaintances, and among them will be some boys and girls you really like, who share a lot of your interests and are fun to be with.

You have a chance to start fresh, to leave behind the things you don't like about where you live now—the teacher who seemed to make a point of asking you the hardest questions; the practical joker in your class who was always playing tricks on you; that group of older kids who hung around in front of the candy store and sometimes blocked the door when you wanted to go in; the neighbors down the street who asked you to run errands for them every time they saw you. What a relief to leave behind all those unpleasant people and situations!

Moving time is also a good time for you to overhaul yourself. Bad habits are hard to break, but being in a new place among new people makes it a little easier to shed them. Teachers and classmates tend to see you as you were when they first knew you; this reinforces patterns of behavior you may have outgrown but which everyone still seems to expect of you. Just because you clowned a lot when you first started school does not mean that you want to be the class comic for the rest of your life; but you will find that your new friends are more willing to take you seriously than the old ones who remember the jokes and pranks you played as a little kid. Or maybe you were very shy a couple of years ago, but now you are ready to step out of the background and be more assertive. You have been growing emotionally and intellectually as well as physically, and moving to another place gives you a great chance to introduce the more grown-up you.

Whether your minus list is longer than your plus list or vice versa, you are already on your way to dealing with the mixed feelings you have about moving. You have identified the things you hate about it, so you can prepare to cope with them. You have also discovered some exciting things about changing homes and can start looking forward to those experiences. You can't avoid all sense of disruption, but you can turn the event into an adventure by keeping cool, being cooperative, and planning ahead.

If you were with your parents when they decided on the house or apartment you will soon be moving to, you already have a general idea of how the place looks. Perhaps you liked it the moment you saw it, or maybe it seemed not nearly as nice as where you live now. How about checking out those first impressions?

Try to have your mother, father, or a grown-up relative spend a few hours with you, getting acquainted with your new home and neighborhood before you move into it. That may be difficult to arrange if you are moving far away, but if you are going to the other side of town, a nearby suburb, or a neighboring city, the chances are you will be able to have a preview.

PREVIEW
2
POST OFFICE
SCHOOL
PARK

An advance look is really worth the time and effort because you will feel more comfortable knowing what your new home and its surroundings look like. You can plan your place in it, which will help you decide what to keep or toss away when you start packing up in your old home. And you can begin to get familiar with the neighborhood, which will make you feel more at home by the end of moving day.

This is a busy time for the whole family, so ask for your preview as far ahead as possible. Set a specific day and time so you won't suddenly have to cancel basketball practice or miss your best friend's birthday party.

BE PREPARED

Think about what you want to find out from this preview, then write it all down in a note book you can comfortably carry with you. Start the list a few days ahead of time and add to it as new questions occur to you.

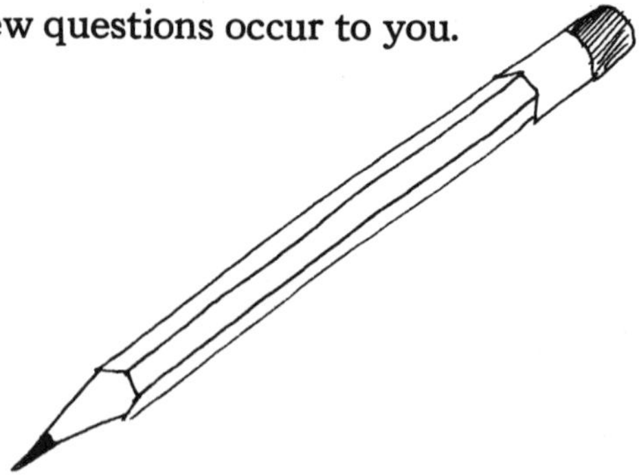

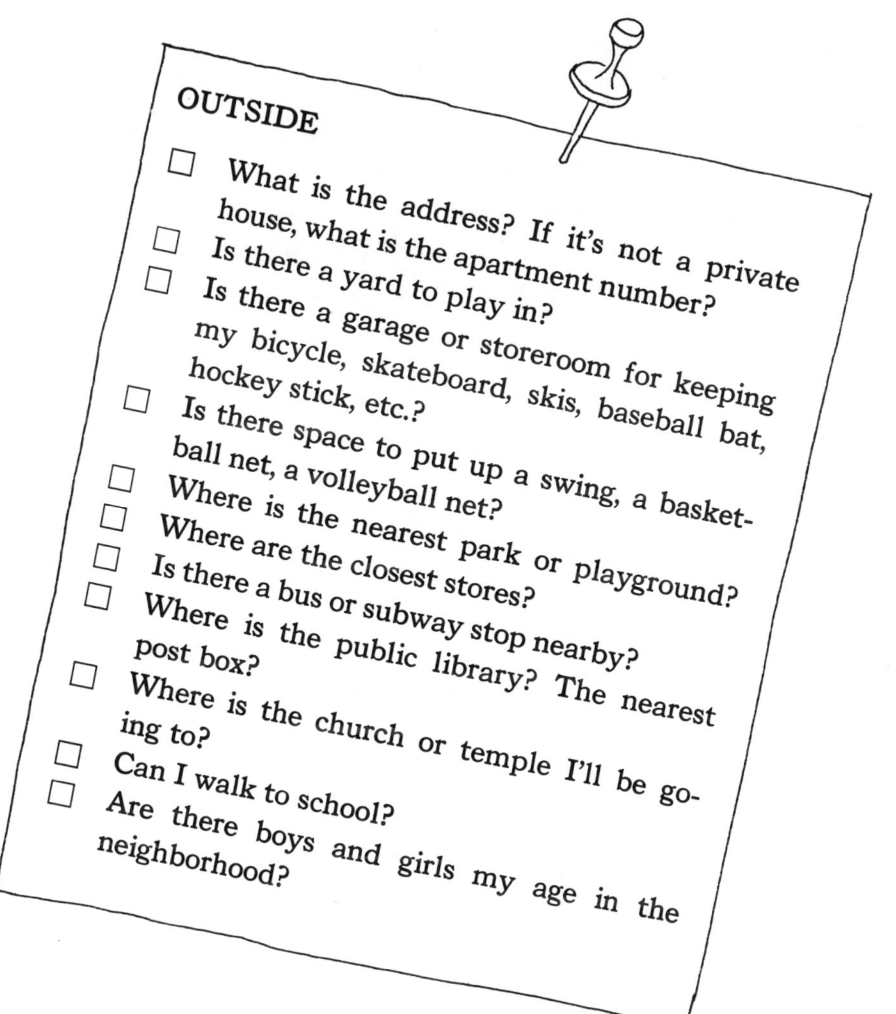

You will be able to answer most of these questions after spending an hour or so exploring the outside of your soon-to-be home and its surrounding neighborhood. Try not to jump to any hasty conclusions about the new place. You are just gathering basic facts now which will give you a head start on feeling at home; but these facts can't even hint at the variety of new people and activities that will soon be part of your life. Moving is unsettling but it can also be an exciting experience if you let it.

INSIDE

- ☐ How many rooms in the house/apartment?
- ☐ What do the windows look out on?
- ☐ Is the kitchen big enough to eat in?
- ☐ Is there a dishwasher?
- ☐ If it is a rented home, are pets allowed?
- ☐ If it is a tall apartment house, how does the elevator work? How does the buzzer system work?
- ☐ Is there a playroom?
- ☐ Which bedroom is mine?
- ☐ Will I be sharing it?
- ☐ How big is my room? ____ feet (____ meters) long by ____ feet (____ meters) wide. How many windows does it have? How many closets? (Make a thumbnail floor plan to remind you where windows, closets, and doors are located.)

WRITE IT DOWN

Don't rely on remembering the answers to these questions. Jot them down in your note-book so you can refer to them in the days ahead when you start to plan and pack.

Be sure to bring a ruler or tapemeasure with you (the retractable kind is handiest) when you go for your preview. You will want to measure your room so you can make a floor plan. Then you can decide where to put things and how you want your new room to look. That kind of planning ahead can be lots of fun and makes it so much easier to get settled once you have moved.

MAKE A FLOOR PLAN

When you get home from the preview visit, mark off the dimensions of your room on a piece of 8½ by 11 inch (21.59 cm × 27.94 cm) paper. Graph paper with ¼ inch (.64 cm) squares is convenient, but plain paper will do as well. Make 1 foot (.3 m) of room space equal to ½ inch (1.27 cm) in your floor plan. If your room is 15 feet (4.5 m) long by 11½ feet (3.45 m) wide, the floor plan will measure 7½ inches (19.05 cm) long and 5¾ inches (14.6 cm) wide. Mark where the windows and entrance and closet doors are. Once you have the basic measurements you can start organizing and arranging what goes into the room.

If you are going to have the room all to yourself, you will have only your own belongings to consider. If you are sharing it with someone else in the family, you had better begin by dividing the floor space into two fairly equal areas. Remember, whoever you are sharing the room with is going to want as much window, wall, and closet space as you do.

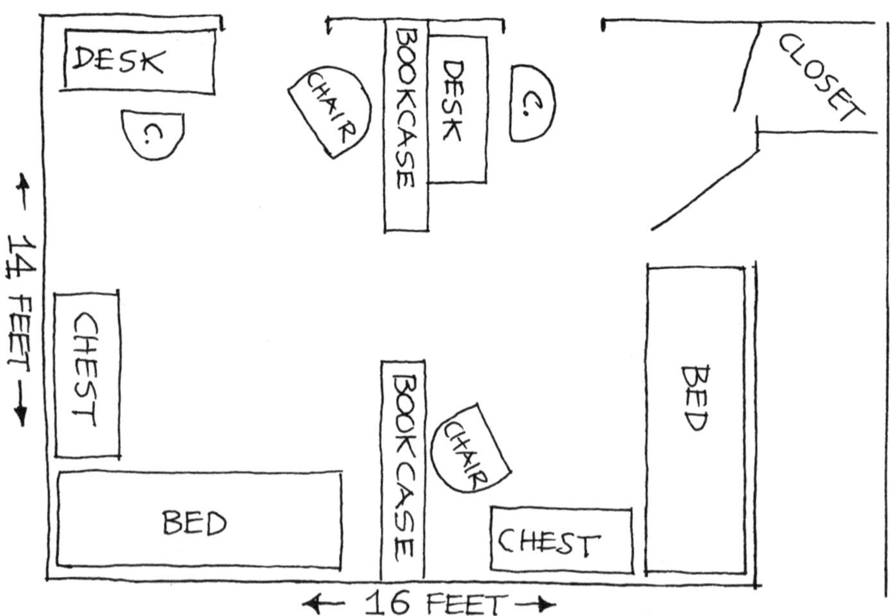

MAKE ANOTHER LIST

What are the things you *must* have in your room?

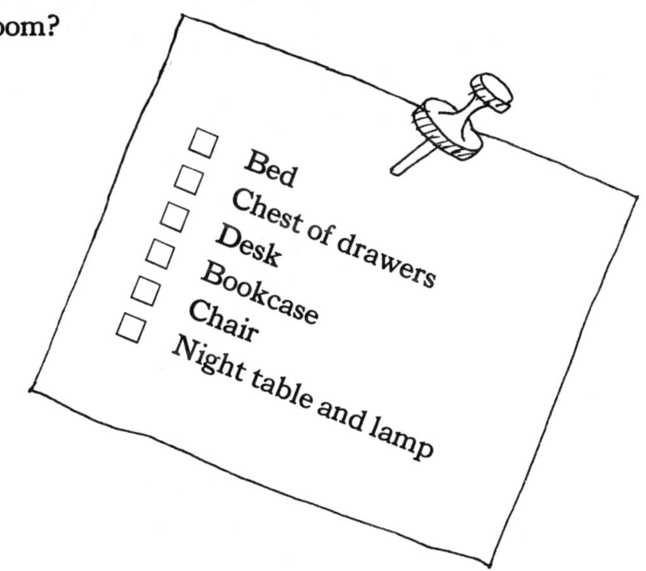

Even some of these may not be necessities. Perhaps your new room has a closet with built-in shelves so you won't need a chest for clothes. Maybe your desk or bookcase can go next to your bed and double as a night table. Making the best use of limited space is challenging but rewarding. The thinking and planning you do at the beginning will give you the sort of room (or part of a room) that fits your own special needs, interests, and personality.

To figure out how to organize the new room, measure the length and width of the basic pieces of furniture. Using the same scale you used to make the floor plan (½ inch = 1 foot [1.27 cm = .3 m]), mark those measurements on a piece of paper and cut them out. Once you have those little squares and oblongs that represent your bed, dresser, bookcase, etc., you can start arranging and rearranging them on the floor plan until you have decided exactly where you want everything placed. It is much easier to move pieces of paper around as you experiment than it is to move the actual pieces of furniture.

If you are sharing the room, you and your roommate should plan together, deciding what space you will use jointly and what space you will want to keep completely personal and private. Here are two floor plans that show how one room can be arranged to give two people comfort and privacy.

Naturally, you will want to let your parents know that you are making plans for your new room, but don't expect them to be interested in each and every decision at this point. They are busy making plans and preparations for getting everything moved, and they are probably a bit tense and preoccupied about the details.

When you have worked out the problems of where to put what, are pleased with the plans (that means both of you if you are sharing a room), and have made a neat, readable copy of the floor plan, then show it to your parents for their approval. And be open to changes they may suggest. Since they have had more experience with this sort of thing than you have, they may have some good ideas that have not occurred to you.

Once the preview is over, it's time to get on to the practical business of moving.

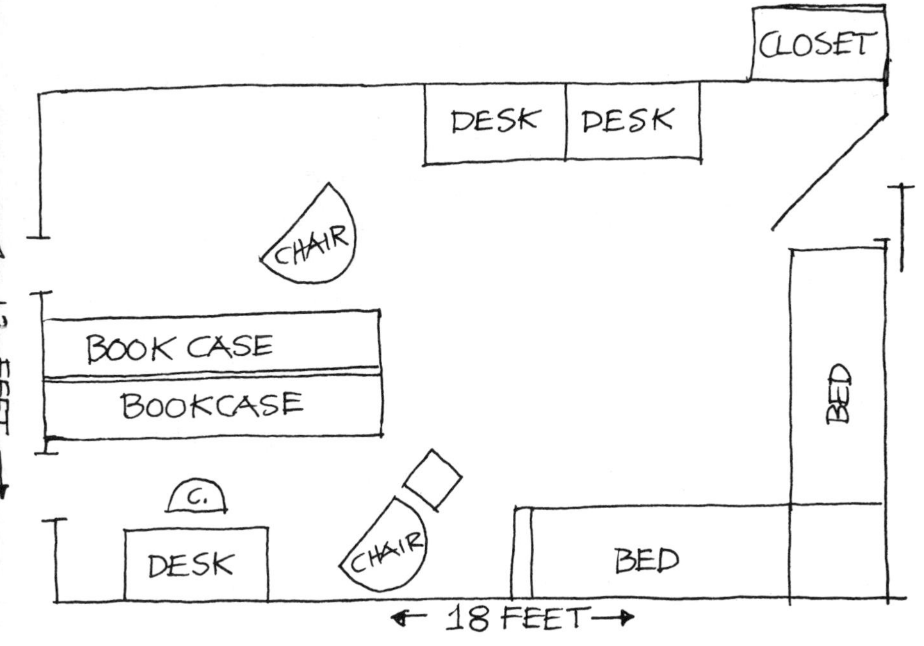

3
GETTING READY
ASSOCIATION
TOYS

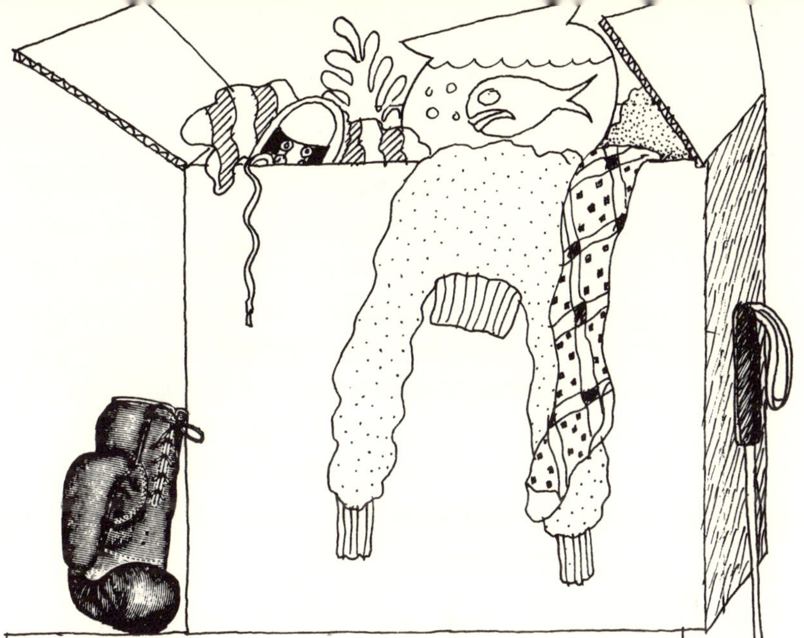

Preparing to move may seem like a mammoth job. There are so many things to think of and do that it is hard to know where to begin. And if you are like most people, your first inclination will be to try to ignore the work ahead and postpone doing anything about it.

Don't give in to that feeling. Don't let yourself delay. Those necessary chores will just hover there in the background, increasing your anxiety and getting in the way of having fun and being productive. So try to get a perspective on what needs to be done. Divide the big jobs into separate, manageable steps. That way you can gauge your progress realistically and know that you are getting things done, slowly but surely.

many boys and girls who works best alone and at your own pace, then don't tackle any moving preparations when people are around. If you share a room with your brother or sister, try to set up a schedule that will give each of you enough time to work alone in the room.

PLANNING YOUR TIME

It has taken you several years to accumulate the stuff in your room, so don't be surprised if it takes you a few hours a day for several days to figure out what to do with all of it. Start the job when you know you are going to have at least an hour or two to work on it. Trying to do it when you have a spare fifteen or twenty minutes only leaves you with a mess and a feeling of discouragement.

For now, everything you absolutely know you will be taking with you can stay in the closet. Everything else should come out of the closet and be put temporarily into a carton, or stacked neatly in an out-of-the-way corner of the room.

A born collector can find a reason for saving just about anything, but those squirrel instincts will only make your moving chores more cumbersome, so try to keep them under control. Each time you are tempted to put something into the "keep" category, ask yourself three questions:

- ☐ Is it usable as is?
- ☐ Have I used it in the last six months?
- ☐ Am I probably going to use it in the next six months?

CLEANING OUT YOUR CLOSET

Do you have a closet that looks like a mini warehouse for the local junkyard? Are your clothes and shoes competing for space with last year's Halloween costume, a box of baseball cards or a sack of marbles that you haven't played with for years, the book bag with your initials stenciled on it that you hate to throw away even though it has a hole in the bottom, a pogo stick you used to hop around on when you were little, or any of the dozens of other odds and ends that find their way into closet corners and seem to multiply of their own accord? If you are a collector, your closet is a good place to start getting ready for the move ahead.

If the answer is no to any two of the three questions, put the item in question in the discard pile for now. You'll have one more chance to reconsider before parting with it forever.

DRESSER DRAWERS AND BOOKCASES

Use the same approach to drawers and bookshelves as you did to your closet, weeding out the remnants of long abandoned hobbies and souvenirs of parties and places you can hardly remember now. What you are taking with you can stay where it is for the time being. In fact, the clothes in your dresser will probably be moved as they are. The moving people usually tie the drawers in place with heavy cord. Since the drawers can't slide open, and clothing is not very heavy, the furniture itself serves as a packing case—one that does not have to be unpacked at the other end of the move. Just be sure to remove anything that might break or spill.

If you have done a conscientious job of weeding out too small tee shirts, comics from two years ago, and books you have already read twice, you are going to have lots of space for new books, games, clothes, and sports and hobby equipment once you are settled in your new home.

Is there any part of your room, any hidden recess, that you have not explored yet? Get to it now so that you can sort through all your discards at one time.

THE NEXT STEP: DIVIDING UP THE DISCARDS

Whether your discard pile is a small, manageable mound or a towering mountain, it probably includes things that someone else would like to have. Divide the discards into two categories—the giveaways and the throwaways.

As you look through all the stuff that you have decided not to take with you, keep in mind that the good sweater you didn't wear very often and outgrew months ago might be just right for your younger brother or sister or for a friend who is smaller than you are. That goes among the giveaways. So do the twice-read books (if they are in reasonably good condition), the chemistry set you just are not interested in any longer, and the jigsaw puzzles you used to love to put together but haven't time for anymore.

On the other hand, no one is going to want a pair of old jeans that are so frayed they are beyond patching, or a catcher's mitt that is in shreds, or a stack of tattered, old *Mad* magazines. Those can be dumped on the throwaway pile.

As soon as you have finished sorting the discards, pack up the throwaways in a carton

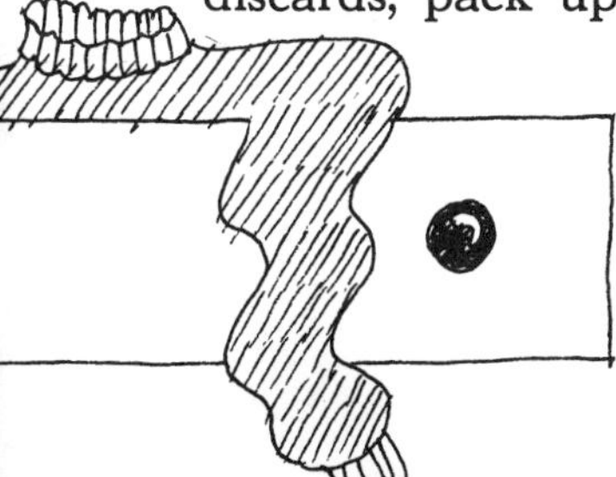

or in sturdy paper or plastic bags. Then get rid of them promptly to avoid confusion and congestion. This last piece of advice comes from Andrew, who reports that he left one carton full of junk in the corner of his room until moving day. The movers got to it before he did, and it ended up being carted off to the new house. That is not a disaster, but it certainly is a waste of space and energy to have garbage moved from one home to another.

Once you are rid of the throwaways, it is time to deal with the giveaways. Here a consultation with your parents is in order since they may have some very definite ideas about what is to be done with those things. If they give you the go-ahead, let your sisters, brothers, cousins, and friends sort through the usable discards and take whatever they want.

There are two other ways of disposing of clothes, toys, furniture, tools, and utensils that are in good condition but that you do not want to take with you. You can have a tag sale for friends and neighbors, or you can donate the things to an organization such as the Salvation Army or Goodwill Industries. If you decide on the donation, your parents will probably want to deduct the value of the gift from their taxes. Whether to have a sale or make a donation is something your parents will have to decide, but there is no reason why either course can't be a joint venture once the decision is made. There may be more exciting things to do than sealing and labeling cartons or putting price tags on items to be sold, but that sort of help, cheerfully given, can go a long way toward soothing the tensions that moving generates.

WHAT TO DO IF YOU HAVE TO LEAVE YOUR PET BEHIND

Sometimes it is not possible to take your dog, cat, gerbil, fish, or bird with you when you move. Perhaps the new landlord will not permit pets, or maybe there will not be enough room in the new home. It is a wrenching experience to leave behind an animal that you have cared for and loved, but if it has to be done, start looking for a new home for your pet as soon as possible.

You can't help feeling sad about giving up a pet, but you don't have to feel anxious about whether it will be well cared for if you and your family give the problem some thought beforehand. Let your friends, neighbors, and classmates know that you are giving away (or selling) a pet because one of them may want to take it.

Type or print an ad on 3 × 5 inch (7.62 cm × 12.7 cm) cards and put the cards up on the bulletin board at school and in appropriate places around your neighborhood—the supermarket, library, community center, "Y," and any other place you can think of. The ad should start with a headline—for example, LOVABLE PET NEEDS HOME—and should include a brief description of the kind of animal it is and its approximate size, age, and sex. Perhaps a few words about its appealing qualities such as affectionate lap cat, good watchdog, intelligent parakeet with ten-word vocabulary, or whatever, would help. Of course, give your phone number so the prospective new owner knows where to reach you.

The people who respond to the ad will probably ask you lots of questions about your pet which you should answer as fully as possible. But remember that you are entitled to ask questions too. You want to find the best home possible for your pet, so you will want to know the following:

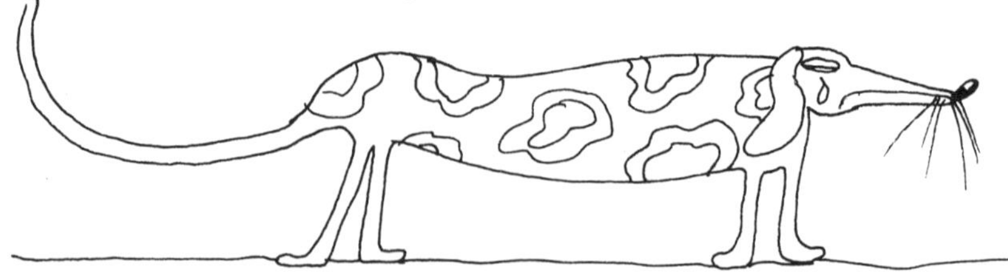

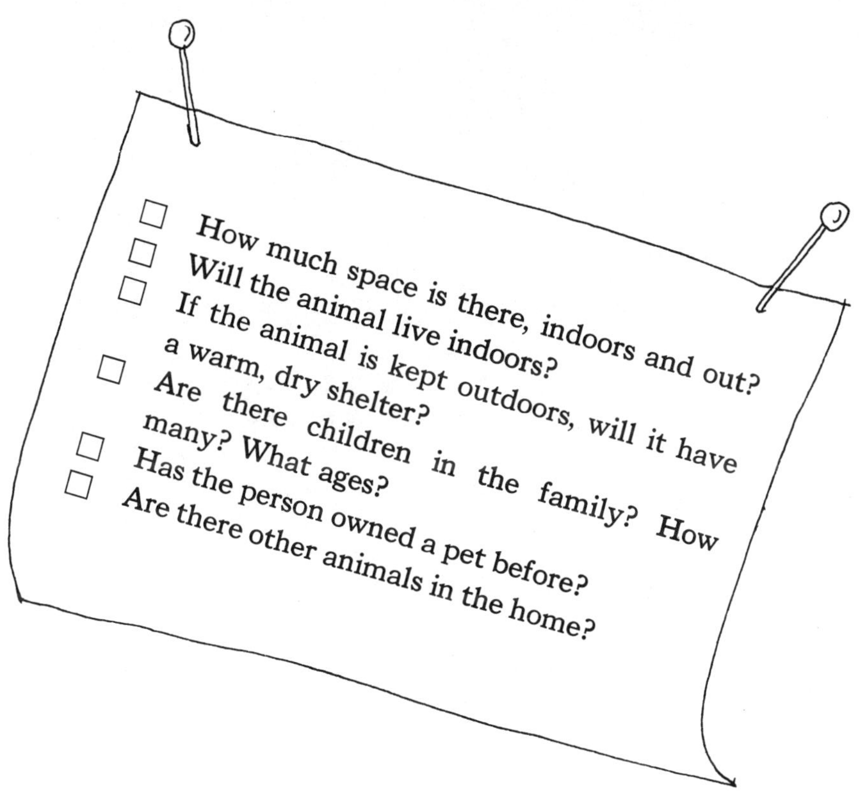

If you and your parents are satisfied with the answers to these questions, then you can arrange to exchange visits. A brief meeting at your house will introduce the prospective owners to the animal. A brief meeting at their home will help you to know if your pet will be happy there. Then you can decide when the animal is to move. If possible, make it a day or two before you do. But that day is still in the future and there are many other things to think about and do now.

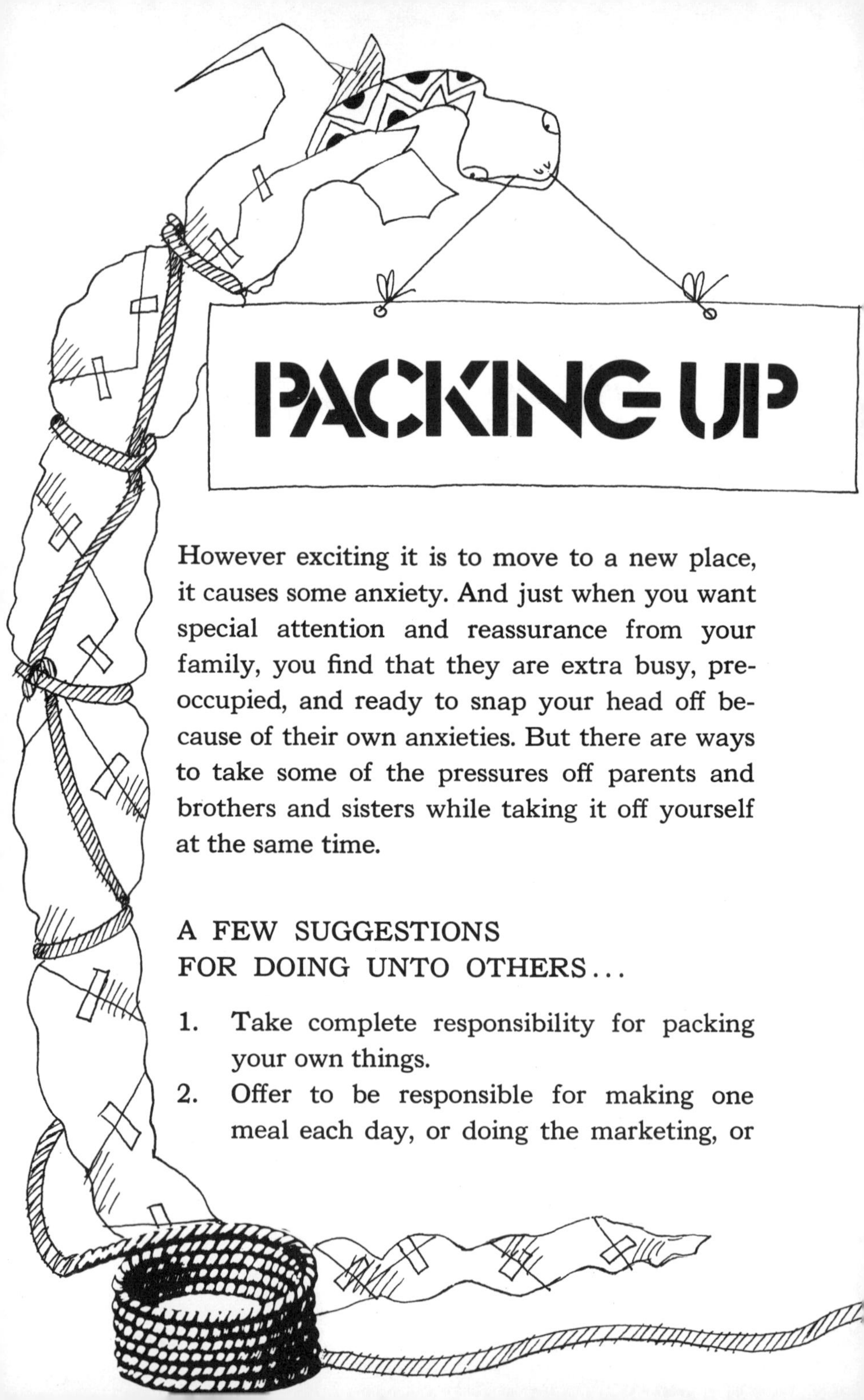

PACKING UP

However exciting it is to move to a new place, it causes some anxiety. And just when you want special attention and reassurance from your family, you find that they are extra busy, preoccupied, and ready to snap your head off because of their own anxieties. But there are ways to take some of the pressures off parents and brothers and sisters while taking it off yourself at the same time.

A FEW SUGGESTIONS FOR DOING UNTO OTHERS...

1. Take complete responsibility for packing your own things.
2. Offer to be responsible for making one meal each day, or doing the marketing, or

HORROR FACES
SMALL THINGS

taking care of your little sister or brother for an afternoon so that your parents can concentrate on their moving chores.

3. Collect cartons. The movers usually supply, for a fee, the large, extra sturdy cartons for packing dishes, glasses, small appliances, kitchen utensils, etc. But for books and personal possessions it is handier to use smaller cartons (approximately 18 inches [45.72 cm] square) that you can get for free from local markets. Liquor cartons are particularly good for packing books in.
4. Set aside an hour a day for helping with general packing—taping and labeling cartons, packing books, wrapping dishes, knicknacks, etc.
5. Offer to be responsible for packing up a particular room, or take care of getting together all the stuff to be donated to church, temple, thrift shop, or wherever.

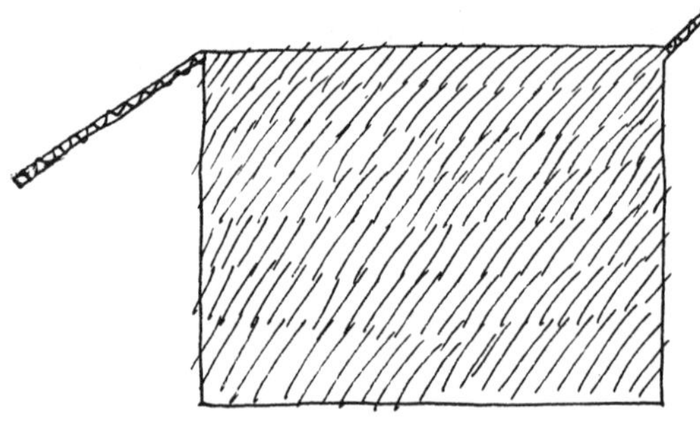

You won't be able to follow all the suggestions in this chapter, and your family will not expect you to. The point is to be generally considerate and as helpful as you can be in specific tasks. You will find that this approach has its rewards. Being an active participant will defuse some of your own anxiety. It will also give you a good feeling of accomplishment, to say nothing of the pleasures of being praised for a job well done.

FIRST THINGS FIRST

Before you get things packed away and out of reach, plan your own personal carry-along survival kit. If reading happens to be your way of getting away from nagging grown-ups, pesky kids, and other problems, then be sure to keep out one or perhaps two books that you really want to read. There probably will be a few hours on moving day when there will be nothing for you to do but wait—for the movers to arrive, to finish loading the van, or to unload the van at the other end. Be prepared with a book to keep your mind off the clutter and clatter about you.

Then again, a portable radio or tape deck may be your favorite way to tune out irritations. Just remember to plug in the earphone attachment since others in the family may not find your hard rock or country and western music as soothing as you do.

Make a list of the other things you will want to carry with you on moving day, and check them off as you gather them together. A zippered tote bag or a drawstring duffle bag will make a handy survival kit. Try to keep it as small and lightweight as possible because you will be carrying it yourself and space will be limited.

Andrew's list included the following:

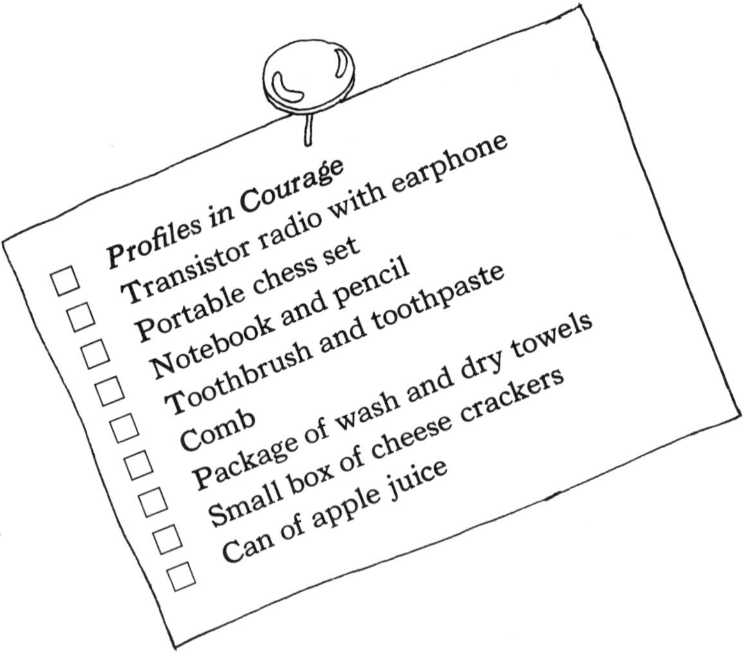

The specific items on your list may be quite different but you will probably want to include the same general categories: something to read and/or listen to, something to play with (a portable board game, a deck of cards, a word game book, etc.), basic one-day needs for personal grooming and hygiene, and something to snack on and quench your thirst with just in case meals are delayed.

GETTING YOUR OWN THINGS TOGETHER

Now that you have disposed of what you do not want to take with you, the time has come to pack. Moving day won't be postponed because you are not ready. It's a good idea to set yourself a schedule and keep to it.

The clothes in chests and dressers can be moved just as they are. The mover will provide wardrobe cartons and any clothes on hangers can simply be transferred from closet to wardrobe just before the move. Everything else has to be packed in cartons so that the moving people can do the job in as few trips as possible from house to van. Movers are usually paid by the hour, so saving time is saving money. The more efficiently you have packed

—consolidating lots of small objects into several large cartons—the more quickly those things can be moved out of your old home and into the new one.

COLLECT YOUR PACKING SUPPLIES

The basic things you will need are several cartons, a roll of 2 inch (5.08 cm) masking tape, a broad-tipped magic marker, scissors, and a big pile of newspapers.

START WITH THE BOOKS

Books are easy to pack because they are flat, unbreakable, and do not need to be wrapped, so why not start by emptying your bookshelves? That will get one chore quickly out of the way.

Be sure the cartons are securely sealed at the bottom. Reinforce them with masking tape if they seem weak. Seal the top flaps with tape as you fill each carton; the top flaps do not have to be as secure as the bottom flaps. Mark the two sides of each carton BOOKS, and mark the top THIS SIDE UP.

CLOSETS NEXT

Continue packing up the unbreakables that include shoes, boots, skates, baseball glove, football helmet, frisbee, and the various other small, sturdy articles and equipment you may have in your closet. Use these guidelines as you go along:

1. Put the heaviest, least breakable things on the bottom.
2. Save space by nesting smaller articles inside larger ones—a ball inside a helmet, for example.
3. Keep things closely packed but not jammed in. A little excess space can always be filled in with crumpled paper to prevent objects from rattling around. Crushed paper is also a good shock absorber to protect breakables.

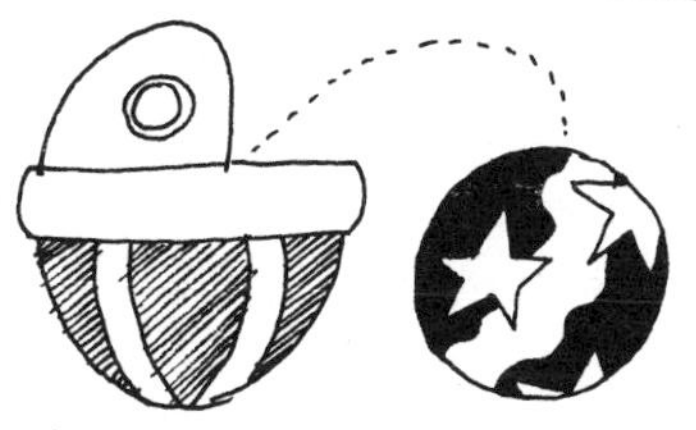

As you fill each carton, tape it closed, clearly mark which side is up, and label it. You don't have to list everything in the carton, but be specific enough to help you identify what is inside each one when you are looking at a sea of similar boxes in the new place. Once you are there (however far off that seems at this moment), you are going to want to make it look like home as quickly as possible. The more organized you are about packing up, the easier it will be to unpack and settle in.

NOW FOR ALL THE OTHER STUFF

By this time you have wrapped and packed enough things to feel pretty confident about how to do it. Now you are ready to tackle all those miscellaneous, odd-shaped objects around the room—jars, bottles, whistles, model cars, figurines, or whatever.

Wrap each item in two or three layers of crumpled newspaper so that all sides are cushioned. Then put a final neatly wrapped layer of paper around it to hold the crumpled paper in place. Fill in small empty spaces in the carton with wads of crumpled paper to keep the objects from rattling around. Again, seal each carton and label it.

PLANTS AND PETS

Living things can't be packed up far in advance, but it does take some planning in advance to move them safely from one place to another. Plants, of course, can get along without your direct attention for several days at a time, so it is a good idea to bring them to the new home a day or two before you move if it is within easy walking or driving distance.

If you have more than a couple of plants, the easiest way to move them is to put as many as will fit into a shallow, medium size carton. A carton 5 inches (12.7 cm) or 6 inches (15.24 cm) deep and 18 inches (45.72 cm) or so square will enable you to carry four or more plants at a time. To keep the pots from sliding and knocking against each other, fill in any gaps with newspaper.

Pets, especially dogs, cats, and birds, often seem to echo their owners' anxieties. They are sensitive to changes in their daily routines and may become a little skittish as moving day approaches. Since you cannot explain to a pet that the disruption is temporary, you can only be reassuring by varying the familiar routine as little as possible, which means remembering to do what you would normally do at the usual time each day, even if your own schedule is haywire.

When you are putting together your own survival kit, it would be a good idea to do the same for your pet. Include a day's supply of food, a food dish, a container for carrying water, and a bowl or cup from which your pet can drink. If you are going to move the animal in a carrier or carton, make sure you have one that is sturdy and roomy. Cats in particular seem to have a sixth sense about an impending change, and they are generally *not* in favor of it. To keep your own temper and your cat's under control, have everything ready in advance.

No one will deny that packing is probably the least rewarding part of moving. Once you have done it, you know it all has to be undone at the other end of the journey; but there is just no way to avoid it. When the packing is finished, though, you are free to concentrate on some of the more interesting offshoots of preparing to live in a new place.

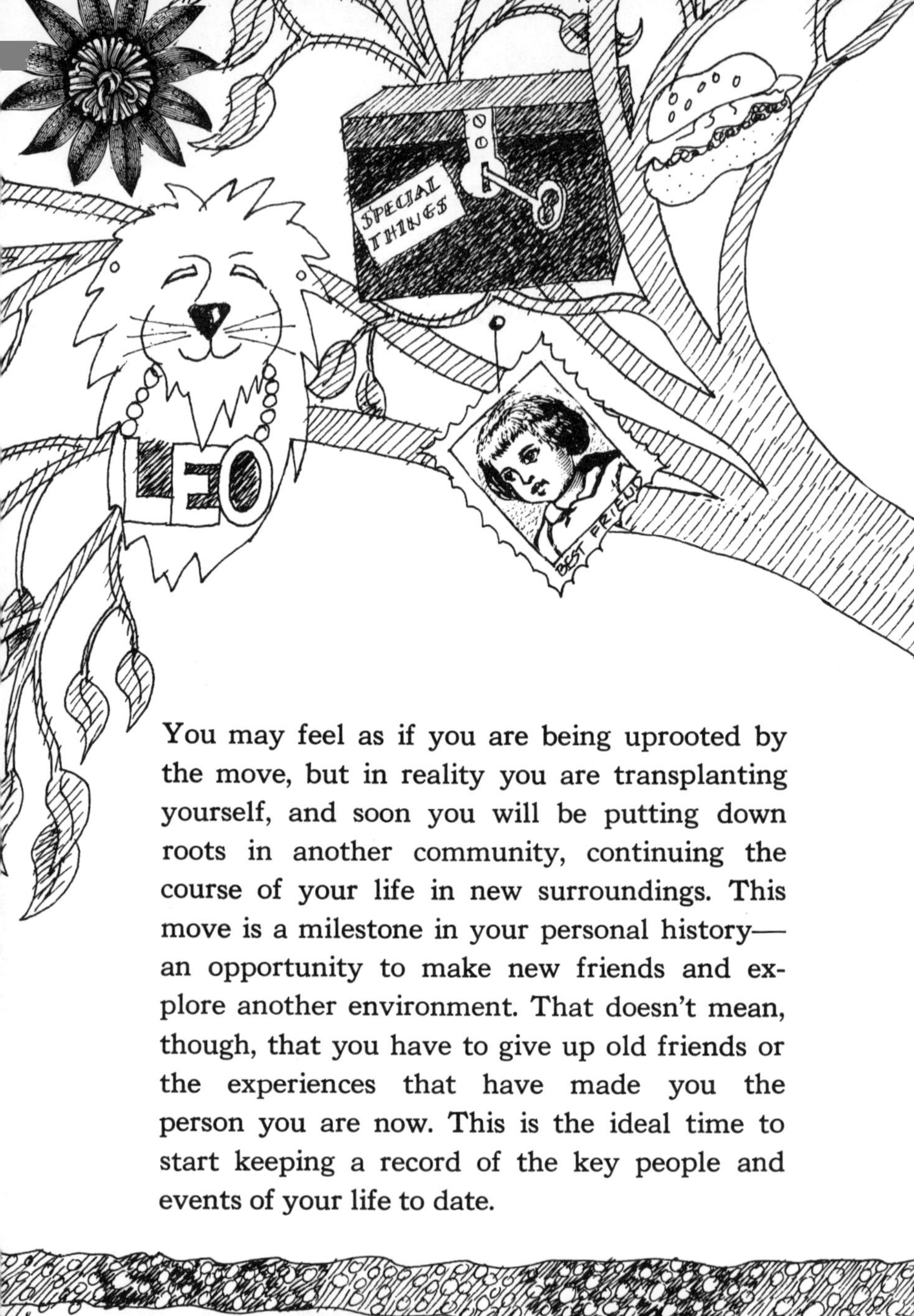

You may feel as if you are being uprooted by the move, but in reality you are transplanting yourself, and soon you will be putting down roots in another community, continuing the course of your life in new surroundings. This move is a milestone in your personal history—an opportunity to make new friends and explore another environment. That doesn't mean, though, that you have to give up old friends or the experiences that have made you the person you are now. This is the ideal time to start keeping a record of the key people and events of your life to date.

TRANSPLANTING

5

YOUR ROOTS

HISTORY IN THE MAKING

No matter how hectic things are while you are getting ready to move, you can find a few minutes here and there to set down the facts of the present before they become half-forgotten memories of the past.

You may think at this moment that you will never forget your friends' birthdays, or your favorite teachers' names, or the addresses of the people you have babysat for almost every week. Don't count on it.

Then again, right now you may not think it is awfully important to remember those things. But in six months you might be embarrassed to find you have forgotten the birthdays of boys and girls who have sent you greetings. Or if the special summer camp program you want to apply for later in the year requires references, you might be out of luck if you can't remember the teachers who have known and liked you for years. Your former teachers can give you more enthusiastic, informative recommendations than new teachers who do not yet know the range of your skills. And when you are looking for an after-school job in your new neighborhood, it is impressive to offer the names and addresses of people who can vouch for your reliability.

Why not start your personal history by writing down the details of your present and your immediate past? You can make it a simple factual record or a journal that includes your feelings and reactions. Just be sure you have it in some permanent form, written on paper or recorded on tape, and not simply floating vaguely in your head.

PAPER VERSUS TAPE

Keeping a written record takes more time than talking into a tape recorder, but it is much easier to look up something in a notebook than to try to find a particular section in the middle of a tape. On the other hand, tape captures the feelings your voice conveys in a way that words on paper cannot do unless you are especially gifted as a writer. On balance, a written journal seems preferable, but if you have a tape recorder, by all means make use of it.

Use a tape recorder as a quick, handy way to record details that can be added to your written journal later; and use it to capture the special rhythms and patterns of your friends' and family's voices. The sound of a person's voice can often recreate that person's personality much more vividly than a whole page of written words. A tape recorder is invaluable, too, when you are interviewing someone because the flow of dialogue is not interrupted or slowed down by the need to take notes.

THIS IS YOUR LIFE

Start with a notebook

Buy yourself an 8 × 10 inch (20.32 cm × 25.4 cm) notebook. You will find that either the spiral-bound or loose-leaf type is handy because the pages lie flat as you write. I feel most comfortable with a spiral notebook, but with a loose-leaf book you can add pages where and when you need them, which is a big plus since a personal history journal can take unexpected twists and turns. You may start with the idea of simply recording basic facts about your friends, relatives, neighbors, and teachers, and then you may find that a cousin's chance remark about some family event recalls a whole flood of memories that you want to put down on paper. With a loose-leaf notebook you can add as many pages as you need to any section of the journal.

If you think that your life just has not been eventful enough to fill more than a couple of 3 × 5 inch (7.62 cm ×12.7 cm) index cards,

FRIENDS

you are in for a surprise. Once you start asking questions of the people around you and exploring your own memories, you will discover how rich and varied your personal history is. You may even decide at some point to follow in Alex Haley's footsteps and trace your background far into the distant past as he did in *Roots*. But for now your focus is the present and the recent past, and your sources are the people around you.

Organizing your journal

Begin by dividing the notebook into general categories such as:

- ☐ Immediate family
- ☐ Relatives
- ☐ School
- ☐ Friends
- ☐ Neighbors
- ☐ Special Interests

These are just suggested headings, of course, and you may want to arrange your book under somewhat different headings. By all means set it up in whatever order and groupings suit you best. This is your personal history; the notebook headings are only useful if they give you a starting point and an efficient way of sorting out and recording information, ideas, and impressions as you go along.

What do you want to know?

Spend a little time thinking about the questions you are going to ask. You are a detective investigating yourself; you want to get the facts straight and complete. Once you move away it will be difficult, if not impossible, to fill in any missing pieces.

Immediate family

This category includes your parents and any sisters and brothers you have. You might think it is silly to put down names, dates, and other facts you already know so well, but it is a good idea to do it just to keep the record complete. Here are some of the basic facts you will want to record:

Full name:
Date and place of birth:
Present address and years of residence:
Previous address and years of residence:
Names and locations of schools attended:
Graduation dates:
Profession:
Place of business:
Date and place of marriage:

Relatives

If you have grandparents or aunts, uncles, and cousins living near you, they should certainly be included in your journal. And you will want to record the same basic information for them as you did for your immediate family. If you want to make note of other facts, such as hobbies, favorite sports, special talents, etc., add those questions to your list.

School

This would include the teachers and other school personnel—principal, dean, guidance counselor, athletic coach, choral conductor, librarian, and others—who have played an important part in your school career to date. Your list of facts should begin, as usual, with the person's full name; but there is no need for you to know his or her date and place of birth, previous address and years of residence, and so forth. The facts you will want to include are:

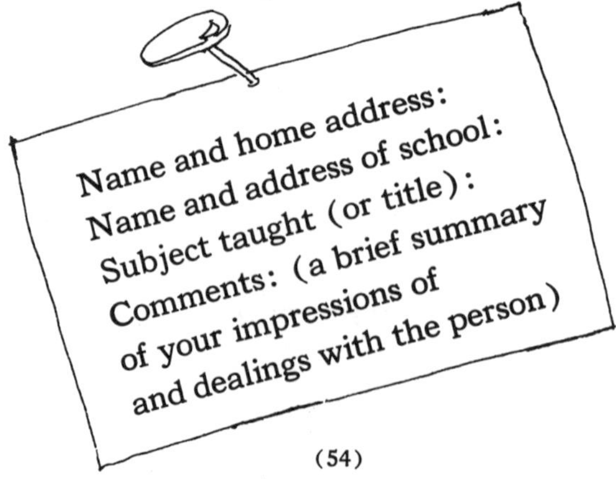

Friends

Since these are the people you have spent the most time with, shared all sorts of adventures with, fought and made up with, and feel particularly sad to leave behind, you will no doubt have a longer list of questions for them. Some of them might be:

Full name:
Address:
Name of school:
Grade level:
Date and place of birth:
Astrological sign:
Number of years you've been friends:
Color of eyes and hair:
Favorite color:
Favorite flower and plant:
Favorite book and author:
Favorite recording stars:
Favorite movie stars:
Favorite TV program and performer:
Hobbies:
Favorite foods:
Best school subject:
Worst school subject:
Future goals:

Neighbors

Because you see them every day, you tend to take for granted the people who live next door or across the street from you. But they are the ingredients that give your neighborhood its particular flavor. In your journal you will surely want to include those you have been friendliest with to help you recall this part of your life after you have moved. Here your notes need not be very detailed:

> Name:
> Address:
> Comments:
> (For example: "Walked the Burtons' Airedale terrier on rainy mornings. Didn't expect to be paid for it, but once a month or so they'd treat my best friend and me to the movies." / "Mr. Warburg loves to bake and he'd bring us a loaf of fresh bread every time he made some for himself." / "Ms. Morelli paints big abstract pictures and invited us to her first gallery exhibit.")

Special interests

If you have interests that have brought you into contact with special teachers, counselors, coaches, and so forth, be sure to add them to your journal. These people might include the clay crafts instructor at the community center, the tennis coach at the "Y," and the person who has been giving you guitar lessons. You will want to note the following information about them:

Name:
Address:
Most important things I learned:

PAST, PRESENT, AND FUTURE

The journal you have begun will give you a firm link with the people and events that are shaping your life. By making a record now, in the present, of key experiences from your recent past, you are creating wonderfully rich source material for further exploration of your roots in the future.

BON VOYAGE

Saying goodbye isn't the end of the world or the end of old friendships. It is the beginning of a new part of your life, which you can share with old friends via letters and visits.

Parting always has some element of sadness in it, but it is also an occasion for celebration. You are going on to make new friends, to have new experiences. This is a time of adventure. You are embarking on a journey, moving from one place to another, and you are moving on to another part of your life. So instead of sulking, how about celebrating this milestone. Have a bon voyage party!

At first thought, it may seem like a crazy idea—having a party when the house is topsy-turvy and everyone is busy with moving chores. But by a day or two before the move, the chances are that whatever has to be done has already been taken care of. And a party is a pretty good incentive for winding up those last-minute tasks a little sooner—in time to enjoy yourself with your friends.

Don't be surprised if your parents are not completely enthusiastic about the idea at first. A party is probably the last thing in the world they want to think about at this point. Just be sure to make it clear that you will take care of all the arrangements before and during the party and any clean-up chores afterward.

INDOORS OR OUT?

No matter what time of year it is, if the temperature is above freezing and the skies are clear an outdoor party is ideal. Here are just a few of the possibilities.

Backyard barbecue

A barbecue is always a paper plate occasion. When the party is over all you have to do is gather up the disposable plates, cups, napkins, and utensils and toss them away. No one gets stuck with washing and drying dishes.

First decide who you are going to ask to your bon voyage barbecue. And plan to limit the guest list to your closest friends. A group of three or four can be great fun, and ten ought to be the absolute maximum. If you invite more than ten, there will be such a crowd that you won't be able to spend much time with any of your guests, and the whole point of this party is sharing the celebration with the people you like best, in order to remember them when you are apart.

Once you know how many people are coming to the party, you will know what you need in the way of paper plates, cups, napkins, eating utensils, and food. If the outdoor grill has not been packed up already, you may want to serve hamburgers and hot dogs. A pound of chopped beef will make four or five hamburgers, so it is easy to judge how much you will need. With hot dogs, of course, all you have to do is count how many there are in a package to know if you have one or several for each guest. The same goes for hot dog and hamburger rolls. And you probably can gauge your friends' appetites pretty accurately.

If there isn't a convenient way to grill the meat outdoors, you can always serve cold cuts and sliced cheese with bread or rolls. If you are having cold cuts, figure that each guest will eat about a third of a pound (150 g). Add a few tasty touches such as sliced tomatoes, hardboiled eggs, pickles, potato chips, mustard, and catsup, plus a variety of soft drinks and cookies or cupcakes for dessert. If you have a fire, have a bag of marshmallows to toast when the coals burn low. Keep the menu simple because you will not have a lot of time to prepare things, and you don't want to have to ask other people in the family to help with your party.

If you would like to have a memento of this farewell party, why not ask your friends to make paper plate self-portraits? Buy enough extra plates to go around, and a supply of grease pencils, felt tip pens, or crayons. Then have everyone draw his or her own face on a plate. When everyone has finished, stack up the plates. Then see if you and your friends can identify who is who. It may not be as easy as you think unless there are some skilled artists in the crowd. Once they have all been identified, have each friend sign his or her self-portrait and you will have an amusing "rogues' gallery" to take with you.

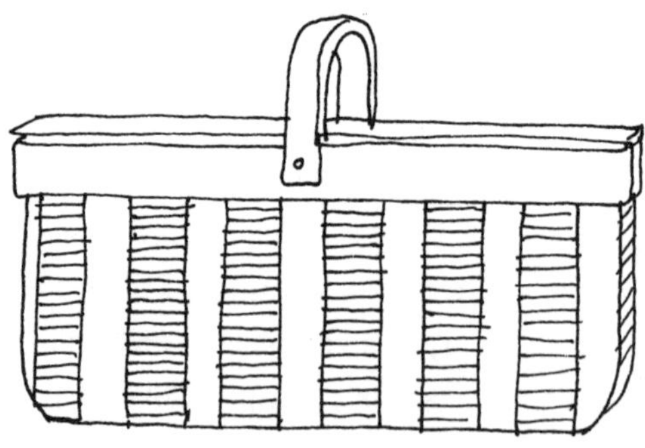

Picnic in the park

If you do not have a backyard, why not have a picnic in a nearby park? You will need the same sort of food and supplies as you would get for a barbecue. Since you will have to carry everything from home to the park, it is a good idea to keep the load as light as possible. The best way to do that is to make the sandwiches in advance and transfer anything in jars to plastic bags. With the sandwiches already made there is no need for paper plates (a big napkin does just as well) or jars of mustard, mayonnaise or relish, or knives for spreading and cutting. Things like pickles, tomatoes, and hardboiled eggs can be treated as finger food. Bring soda in lightweight cans rather than in bottles. And, of course, be sure no litter has been left about when the picnic is over.

Take along a frisbee and a couple of kites. A kite-flying contest can be quite a challenge with two teams of two people each competing to see who can get the kite into the air first. And everyone at the party can join in a fast frisbee game.

Beach party

If the day is sunny and warm, and you live near the ocean or a lake, have your picnic on the beach. Again, bring along a frisbee, kites, or a beachball. Building a giant sand castle and hunting for beautiful shells are always fun to do.

Partying indoors, in the middle of the mess

Suppose the weather does not cooperate, and rain or the midwinter temperature makes outdoor eating impossible. Well, there is always the house. Cartons may not be elegant, but they make perfectly adequate seats and table tops. A few crepe paper decorations and clusters of brightly colored balloons will give the place a festive air. Again, picnic food and paper plates are in order.

Perhaps you have not played hide and seek since you were little, but all the unexpected nooks and crannies created by cartons and topsy-turvy furniture make wonderful hiding places, so you may not be able to resist having one last game. If you think, though, that an active game would be more than the other members of your family could cope with, there are lots of entertaining things you can do within the confines of one room.

A silly songfest will keep everyone giggling. Have one person start by singing the first three or four bars of a song. The next person has to pick up where the first stopped, singing a different song with a lyric that begins with the same word that the previous song ended with. You are sure to come up with some strange and funny hybrids.

Another way to do silly singing is to substitute a nonsensical word for the actual one at the end of every other line. If you have a tape recorder don't forget to use it while everyone is singing.

How about making a group poem, with everyone contributing a couplet? Give each person a piece of paper to write on, and after everyone has read his or her lines, put the poem together with tape or glue. Then if you are near a store or a library with a duplicating machine, make a copy for each person to have as a memento of your bon voyage party.

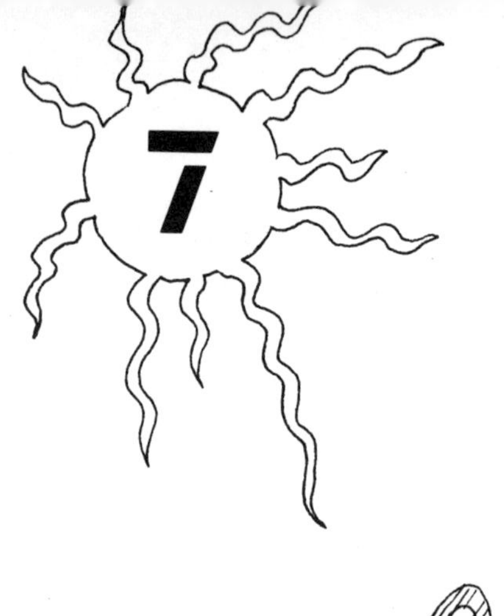

7

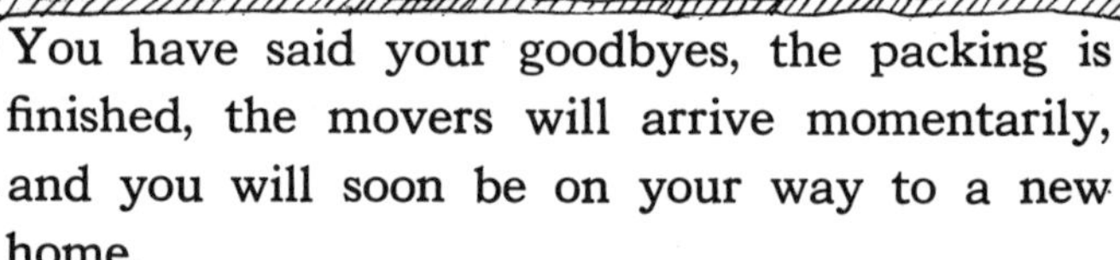

You have said your goodbyes, the packing is finished, the movers will arrive momentarily, and you will soon be on your way to a new home.

This is not a morning for lolling in bed, so be sure to get up promptly and get ready. Today there will be no choices to make about what to wear. Everything but what you will need for the day has been packed away. This is one morning when the bed does not have to be made; just strip it of sheets and blankets and leave it for the mover to deal with.

The whole place is probably so disorganized that it seems strange and almost unfamiliar. And however uncomfortable that may make you feel, it has one definite advantage. Now that home is no longer very homey, it is

MOVING
MORNING

not so hard to leave. With the rugs rolled up, every footstep clatters against the bare floors. You can see that the walls need painting now that the pictures are down, and the window sills look forlorn without plants lined up along them. Now for the first time perhaps, you may start looking forward to getting away from where you are and settling into the new place.

FIRST THINGS FIRST

Once you have brushed your teeth, washed, and put on your clothes, pack any last minute additions in your carry-along survival kit and put it where you can get it easily when you are ready to leave. Don't let it get mixed up with the cartons and furniture that the movers will be loading in the van. And remember to keep it as compact as possible. If you are going to be traveling by bus, train, or plane, the less you have to carry, the more comfortable the trip will be. If you are going to the new place by car or taxi, space will be limited and you will have to share what there is of it with the rest of the family.

If you are moving with a pet, make sure you have packed up everything it will need for the day, and put the pet's survival kit with your own.

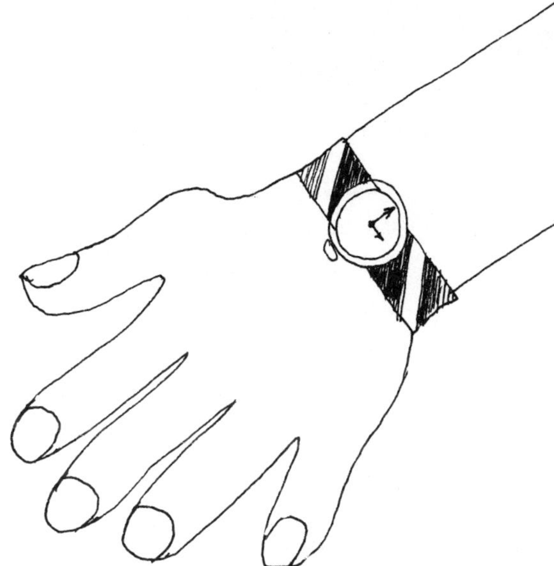

LEND A HAND

Once your personal chores are out of the way, try to help wherever needed. A hearty breakfast is definitely in order on moving morning so if you are handy in the kitchen, by all means offer to make breakfast. Of course, all the utensils for cooking and eating may already be packed away, but that does not mean your family has to go without a morning meal. Unless you live way out in the country, there is probably a place nearby where you can buy ready-to-eat food.

To avoid hunger pangs and the short tempers that come with them, appoint yourself chief cook or breakfast buyer. And while you are in the kitchen, get together any food your family wants to take along for later in the day —snacks, a thermos of hot soup or coffee, or the makings of a picnic lunch.

If kitchen duties and food shopping are activities that you think are as unappealing as doing homework, find other ways to make yourself useful. There are lots of possibilities. Keeping younger members of the family quietly entertained is something your parents will appreciate. Or offer to make one last tour of the house, checking closets and corners to be sure nothing is left behind.

And if there is nothing left to do in the last hour or two before leaving, take yourself off to the most comfortable, out-of-the-way corner, with a good book or a transistor radio. Keep the radio volume low or, better yet, use an earphone so your rock music doesn't rock your parents' tempers.

Once the movers have come and gone, leaving your old home empty and echoing, it is time to gather up your few remaining personal belongings, say a final goodbye to the place, and start looking forward to new adventures.

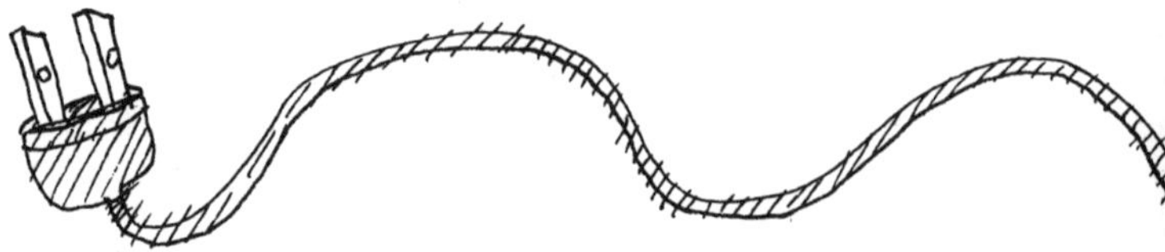

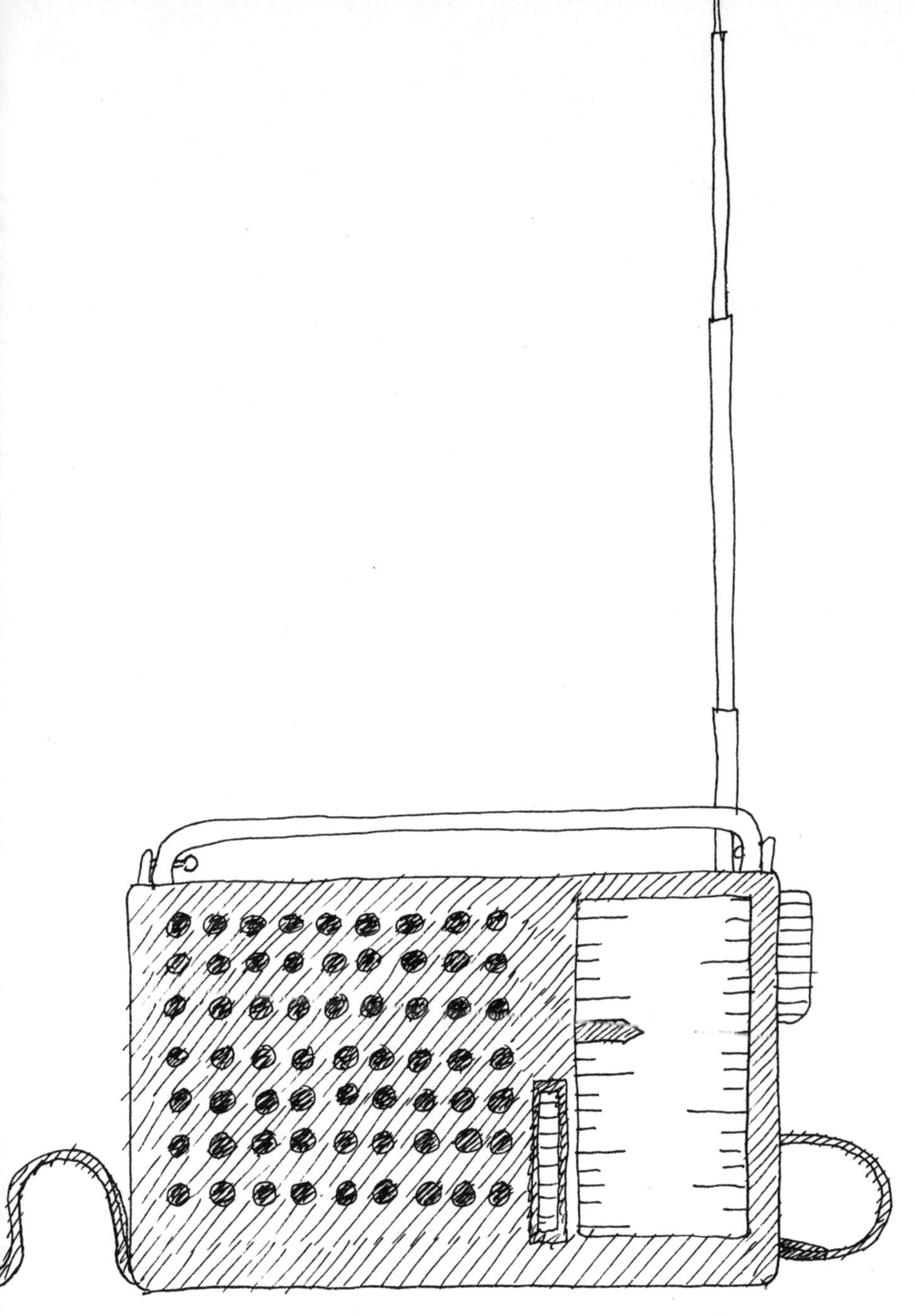

GETTING
SETTLED
8
STUFF

Whether the move has taken you a few miles or half a continent away, the immediate results are the same. You have been uprooted and set down in a place of semiorganized clutter. Complaining will not improve the situation, so you might as well make the best of the temporary confusion. It won't last forever and it can even be fun for a little while. No matter how much you may have hated to leave your old home, there is something irresistibly exciting about exploring and getting to know a new living space.

If you have a pet, one of the first things to do is to look after its needs. Fill the animal's water dish immediately. Put it where it can be reached easily, but be sure it is out of the way of traffic so it will not be knocked over. If you have a dog, take it out for a short walk as soon as possible, and walk it more frequently than usual for the first day or two. Even the best trained dog may have an accident in the confusion and excitement of changing homes. If you have a cat, put down its litter box right away. Again, put it where the cat can get to it easily but where people will not be tripping over it. Having the favorite old towel, blanket, or cushion that your cat or dog likes to sleep on will convince the animal that this unfamiliar new place is really home.

If you have caged pets, be sure to put the cage where there is likely to be the least noise, activity, and confusion—in a quiet corner away from drafts. Moving is as tiring to animals as it is to humans.

BOXES, BOXES EVERYWHERE

For the first day or two you are going to be awash in a sea of cartons. But if you and the rest of the family did a good job of packing and labeling, you will know which cartons belong in which rooms, and that will make the job of unpacking and putting things away go much faster. But you do not have to wait until everything is unpacked to begin to feel at home.

EIGHT QUICK WAYS TO MAKE YOURSELF AT HOME

1. Your carry-along survival kit has done its job, but don't just dump it amid the confusion of cartons. Bring it directly into your room when you arrive so you will know where to put your hands on at least one book, one game, or a radio until your other things are unpacked. Reading a book or listening to music are good ways of tuning out the chaos around you when there is nothing much for you to do.

2. Take your clothes out of the moving carton right away and hang them in your closet. Just seeing some of your own familiar things in place will help you to feel that you are really at home.

3. Put your favorite picture or poster on your bedroom wall. The room will immediately look more welcoming. And if you have already designed the layout of the room using a floor plan you made before moving, you will know just where you want the picture to go.

4. Set up your bedside lamp right away. If you do not have any place to put it for the moment, use a packing carton as a night table. In a strange new place it is reassuring to have a

light within arm's reach. And it is nice to have the cozy glow of a table or floor lamp rather than the harsh glare of a ceiling light.

5. Put your book or radio next to the lamp near your bed. Then if you wake up in the middle of the night and can't fall asleep again, you will have something to take your mind off the strangeness of being in an unfamiliar place. Chances are, though, that you will sleep soundly through that first night after the hectic activity of moving day.

6. Get to know your front door. That may sound silly, but if you were to close your eyes and try to visualize the approach to your new home you probably couldn't, although you had arrived there only a few hours ago. In that flurry of fatigue and curiosity, with your parents leading the way and taking charge of the keys, you may not have noticed the general location and appearance of the entrance to your new home. Of course you know the number so you can identify it that way, but it will

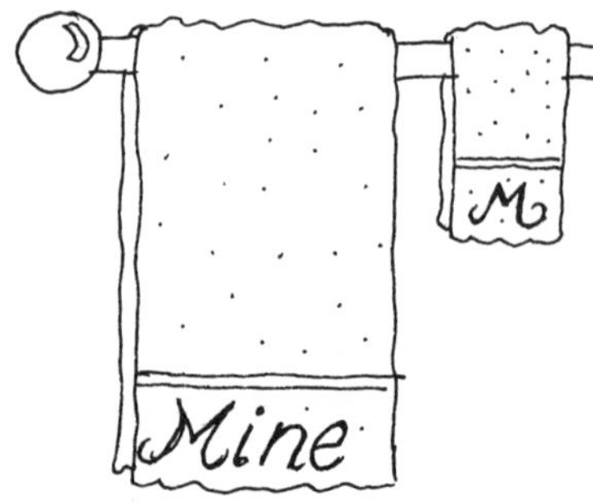

only really *feel* like home when it begins to *look* familiar. So find some good reasons to go in and out a few times that first day. As the unpacking proceeds someone is sure to need picture hooks, a screwdriver, a can opener, or a container of milk. Running a few errands will give you a head start on getting to know the new neighborhood.

7. Stake out your space in the bathroom. The morning after you arrive, when you are eager to start unpacking and settling in, you will be glad not to have to hunt around for a towel, a toothbrush, toothpaste, and a comb.

8. Take a long, careful look out of each window in your new home. Make a mental note of what catches your attention first from each vantage point. Then, during the first day or two, go out and explore up close the things that rouse your interest and your curiosity. The sooner you get to know your immediate surroundings, the sooner you will feel at home in them.

Andrew and his parents had moved in early spring before the trees had any leaves on them. One of the things that intrigued Andrew as he wandered from room to room looking out of windows in his new house was a big old apple tree. The apple tree was near a tall hedge dividing his yard from the neighbors' yard. The lower branches were gnarled and almost horizontal, making it ideal for climbing, which he wasted no time in doing. As he was hoisting himself up he heard a familiar rhythmic *whoosh-thunk* sound, and when he got up higher than the hedge he saw the girl next door hitting a tennis ball against the rear wall of the garage. She spied him a moment later and waved, saying that she was glad to see someone in that great climbing tree because the people who lived there before had not let anyone near it. Andrew invited her to come over and try it herself, and he made a friend that first morning he started exploring his new neighborhood.

TEAMWORK FIRST

For the first few days after you arrive you probably will not have much time to devote to your purely personal concerns. Since everyone uses the kitchen, bathroom, and living room, the whole family is going to feel a bit unsettled until those rooms are in order. It is worth postponing designing and decorating plans for your own room to pitch in and help with family chores. There are lots of ways you can lend a hand, and perhaps at the same time keep younger sisters or brothers busy and useful too. Here is a basic checklist, but don't hesitate to add to it:

- ☐ cleaning and lining kitchen cabinets and drawers
- ☐ unwrapping, washing, and drying kitchen utensils
- ☐ unwrapping, washing, and drying dishes, glasses, and silverware
- ☐ unwrapping and cleaning small kitchen appliances
- ☐ cleaning the stove or the refrigerator (ghastly chores, but someone has to do them)
- ☐ filling the salt shaker, peppermill, and sugar bowl
- ☐ filling the ice cube trays

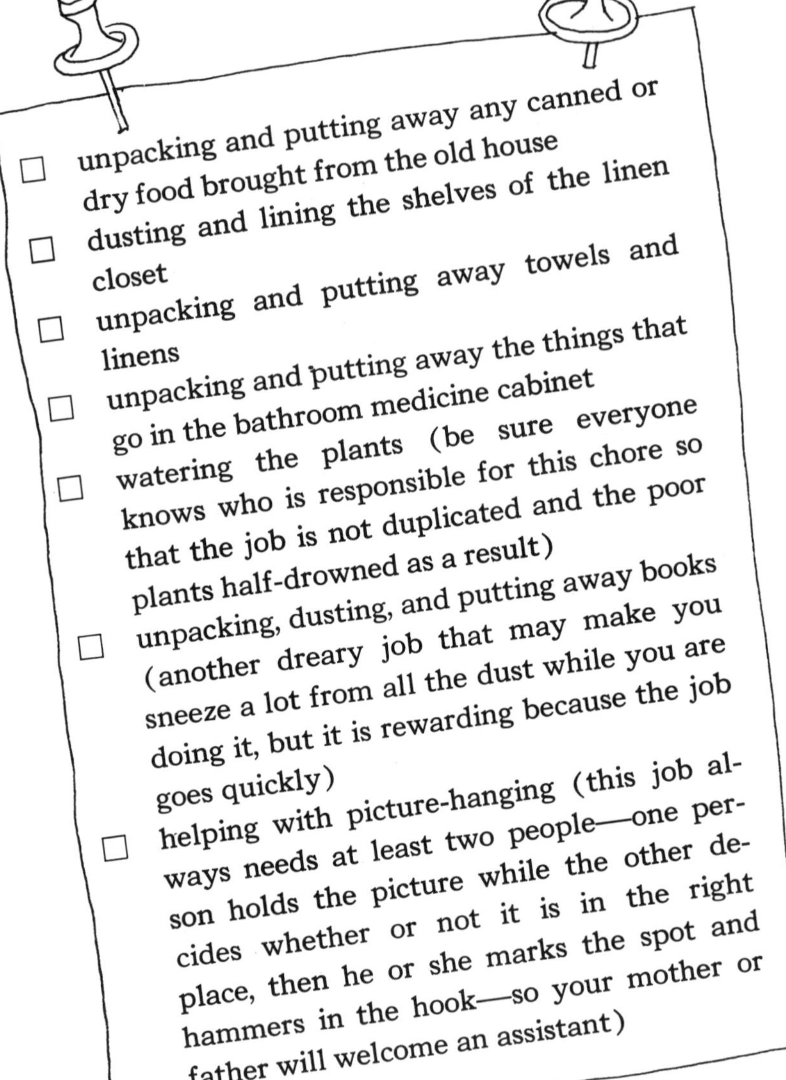

- ☐ unpacking and putting away any canned or dry food brought from the old house
- ☐ dusting and lining the shelves of the linen closet
- ☐ unpacking and putting away towels and linens
- ☐ unpacking and putting away the things that go in the bathroom medicine cabinet
- ☐ watering the plants (be sure everyone knows who is responsible for this chore so that the job is not duplicated and the poor plants half-drowned as a result)
- ☐ unpacking, dusting, and putting away books (another dreary job that may make you sneeze a lot from all the dust while you are doing it, but it is rewarding because the job goes quickly)
- ☐ helping with picture-hanging (this job always needs at least two people—one person holds the picture while the other decides whether or not it is in the right place, then he or she marks the spot and hammers in the hook—so your mother or father will welcome an assistant)

Once these settling-in chores are out of the way, the place will begin to look and feel like home. Meal schedules will be back to normal; you won't be tripping over boxes and cartons; the living room couch and chairs will emerge from under dust covers; and you will know where to look when you want a glass, a spoon, a book, or a Band-aid. Now it is time to concentrate on you.

CREATING YOUR

Whether you have a bedroom all to yourself or you are sharing it with another member of the family, you have a brand new space to settle into. Now is the time to make that space exactly what you want it to be.

To decide how you want the room to look, it is important to know what you want to use it for. Here are a few questions to ask yourself before arranging furniture, pictures, and playthings.

1. Is this a room for just changing clothes and sleeping? If that is the case, your main concerns will be how to organize closet and drawer space most conveniently, and where to place the bed for maximum comfort—near or far from the radiator/air conditioner, facing

OWN SPACE
9

toward or away from the window. If you like to lie in bed and look out of the window before falling asleep at night, you will want the bed in one location; and if the morning light wakes you too early, you will want it in another location.

2. Is this a room where you will be doing your homework and most of your reading and listening to music? In that case you will want to arrange the space so you have enough room for a desk or table to write on, a sturdy chair to use at the desk, a cozy, comfortable chair for pleasure reading, good light at both the desk and the reading chair, and a cabinet suitable for holding books, records or tapes, a record player or a tape deck, and a radio.

3. Is this a room where your friends will gather when they come to see you? (Yes, you will have friends here soon, however remote the possibility seems now.) If you think you will want to provide sitting space for several people at a time, it would probably be a good idea to place the bed against a wall and treat it as if it were a studio couch. A couple of large pillows with sturdy covers will make sitting on the floor more comfortable.

4. Is this a room that will double as a work-

room for your hobby? Then you will have to take into consideration what sort of space and equipment that activity requires. Sewing and kite making will certainly require more space than doing needlepoint or writing stories. Keep in mind, too, the sort of storage space you will need for your hobby materials or tools. You will not want to look at those things all the time, so think of ways to keep them neatly out of sight when you are not using them. A large cardboard box that slides under the bed is a good solution if closet and drawer space are limited.

5. Is this a room that has to be shared with someone else who has different needs and tastes than yours? You are both entitled to privacy and there are ways to make a single room into pleasing individual spaces for two or, if necessary, three people. Take another look at the floor plans on pages 18 and 21 to get an idea of how to go about this.

Don't forget the closet when you start dividing up space. If there is only one closet to be shared by two people, keep clothing separate by wrapping a long piece of colorful cord around the middle of the clothes rod. A touch of epoxy glue will keep it from sliding to the left or right. Take the long end of the cord and attach it with a tack to either the floor of the closet or to the shelf above the rod. Then you can tell at a glance whether or not you are within your boundaries. Shoe bags that hang on the inside of the door are a handy way of keeping shoes off the floor. A standard size door will hold two six-pair shoe bags hung one above the other.

Small high-intensity reading lamps are good to use in shared space. They provide a lot of light but are focused in a narrow range. You can stay up late reading or doing homework without disturbing your roommate's sleep, even if he or she is sensitive to light.

You can have a radio and a phonograph going at the same time too—if both listeners use earphones.

If you are sharing a room, cooperation is the key. Give it generously and make it clear to your roommate from the beginning that you expect equal consideration on his or her part. Age should not convey any special privileges. On the other hand, if one of you loves having plenty of space to spread out in, and the other is content in a small, cozy area, there is no reason to insist on exactly equal division of space. This is something to consider even if you and your brother or sister have your own rooms. If there is a choice of rooms, try to decide who takes which room on the basis of needs rather than status.

Judith, age eleven, and her sister Ann, age thirteen, recently moved from a Long Island suburb to a three-bedroom apartment in New York City. Two of the bedrooms are large and one is quite small. The girls' parents took one of the large rooms and let Judith and Ann decide how the two other rooms would be used. At first they considered sharing the large bedroom and making the small one into a recreation room to use when their friends were visiting, or to retreat to when their parents had guests and they did not feel like joining the grown-ups in the living room.

But after thinking about the differences in their personalities and habits, they decided against sharing a room. Ann is methodical and well-organized, and she likes having every detail of her surroundings in good order. She makes and collects miniatures, and she enjoys an intimate space with lots of natural light. Judith is much more casual (Ann calls it sloppy). Her belongings have a way of distributing themselves over the widest possible area. She likes a maximum of space and a minimum of furniture.

Choosing the right rooms was not difficult. Although Ann, as the older sister, could have insisted on the large room, she preferred the small one that had corner windows facing east and south. Judith took the large back bedroom where she has two long walls to hang the travel and rock concert posters she collects, and she also has lots of floor space for doing yoga exercises.

Since there are two bathrooms in the apartment, Ann and Judith share one of them. After a few days of mixed-up towels, toothpaste, shampoo, and complexion soap, the girls decided they had to divide the space and keep their various paraphernalia within those territorial boundaries. Ann made a bunch of As and Js out of colorful masking tape and used them to identify the appropriate toothbrush holders, towel racks, and shelf space.

This is a handy way of keeping bathroom belongings straight when two people share the facilities, and it is a virtual necessity when more than two people use the same bathroom. If you, your parents, and one or more sisters or brothers share a bathroom, why not suggest a division of territory and offer to make the initials to label whose belongings go where?

TRANSLATING THE FLOOR PLAN INTO REALITY

If you had a chance for a preview of your new home, you probably made a floor plan of your room before moving. After being in the place for a couple of days and giving more thought to how you want to use your room, you may have changed the original plan somewhat. Now is the time to put the plan into action.

You still have a number of cartons of books and other belongings to be unpacked, but there is no point in doing that until the furniture is in place. For the time being, put all the cartons in one corner or against a wall where you are pretty sure you won't put any furniture.

Now look at your floor plan to see just where your bed, dresser, bookcase, desk, and other furniture should go. You will probably need some help in putting the furniture in place. Most of it is too heavy to be lifted by one person, and pushing or pulling a bulky piece may scratch the floor. Once everything is in place, don't be surprised if it does not look exactly the way you imagined it would. It is hard for anyone but an experienced interior designer to be able to visualize how a room will actually look based on a two-dimensional floor plan. Try not to be discouraged or impatient. Instead, try to analyze what you dislike about the arrangement and why. Perhaps your desk, which seemed to fit so nicely into a corner on the floor plan, feels too closed-in and cramped now that it is actually in place. If that is the case, ignore that part of the floor plan and experiment a little. Put the bookcase where you had planned to have the desk, and move the desk to the wall that the bookcase was against.

It is worth spending a little extra time now to try to make the room as close to your ideal as possible. This may be the first time you have had a chance to design a part of your living space. The more the room fulfills your needs and expresses your personality, the more comfortable and at home you are going to feel in it.

Once you have the furniture arranged for maximum convenience and eye appeal, you are ready to finish the last of the settling-in chores. All those cartons of personal belongings you carefully packed a week or so ago now have to be unpacked and put away. Unpacking is not nearly so tedious as packing and, hallelujah, when that is out of the way you will know that moving time is truly over!

LETTING YOURSELF SHOW THROUGH

Most rooms are rectangular, with windows on one or two walls, an entrance door, and a closet or two. Most bedroom furniture is pretty standard too. It is not the room itself, or even the basic furniture you have in it, that makes it a special place that expresses your personality. It is the things you choose to surround yourself with, and the way you organize them, that makes your room (or your part of a room) a personal statement. So let the space and the objects reflect who you are, and who you are striving to be.

If you could not bring yourself to throw away certain things when you were packing to leave, reconsider now. Do they seem unnecessary or out of place in the new room? Don't let products of old, abandoned hobbies take up space you want to use for new interests. If making and displaying model planes no longer appeals to you, don't clutter up your room with the collection because it has become a habit. And there may have been a time when you didn't mind that your collection of miniature animals took up two whole shelves in the bookcase, but lately you have lost interest in them. They are a pain in the neck to dust, and you need those shelves for your growing stack of books. Think about keeping a few of those miniatures on your dresser or your night table and giving the rest to a younger brother, sister, or cousin.

If you have grown up with green and flowering plants around the living room, dining room, family room, and kitchen, perhaps you thought of them only as a nuisance when you were asked to water them. But think again, and you may decide that a few pots of hardy plants like pothos and philodendron will give your room a bright, fresh, outdoorsy look that more than compensates for the minimal attention they require. You might want to try some kitchen scraps gardening too, experimenting with grapefruit, orange, and lemon seeds, avocado pits, pineapple tops, and those sorts of things to see what plants develop.

Those freshly painted walls need some colorful decorations, but don't feel you have to fill every inch of space. By the time you had moved, perhaps you were tired of looking at the faces of last year's favorite television stars or football greats or country and western singers tacked up on your walls. Maybe you are ready to hang a few handsome travel posters, a beautiful kite or two, or some inexpensive prints of famous paintings.

Hobbies and pictures that suited you perfectly a year or two ago may seem like kid stuff now. Go with your new feelings and interests. You are growing and changing, so let your new room express the new you.

FEELING AT
HOME AGAIN
10

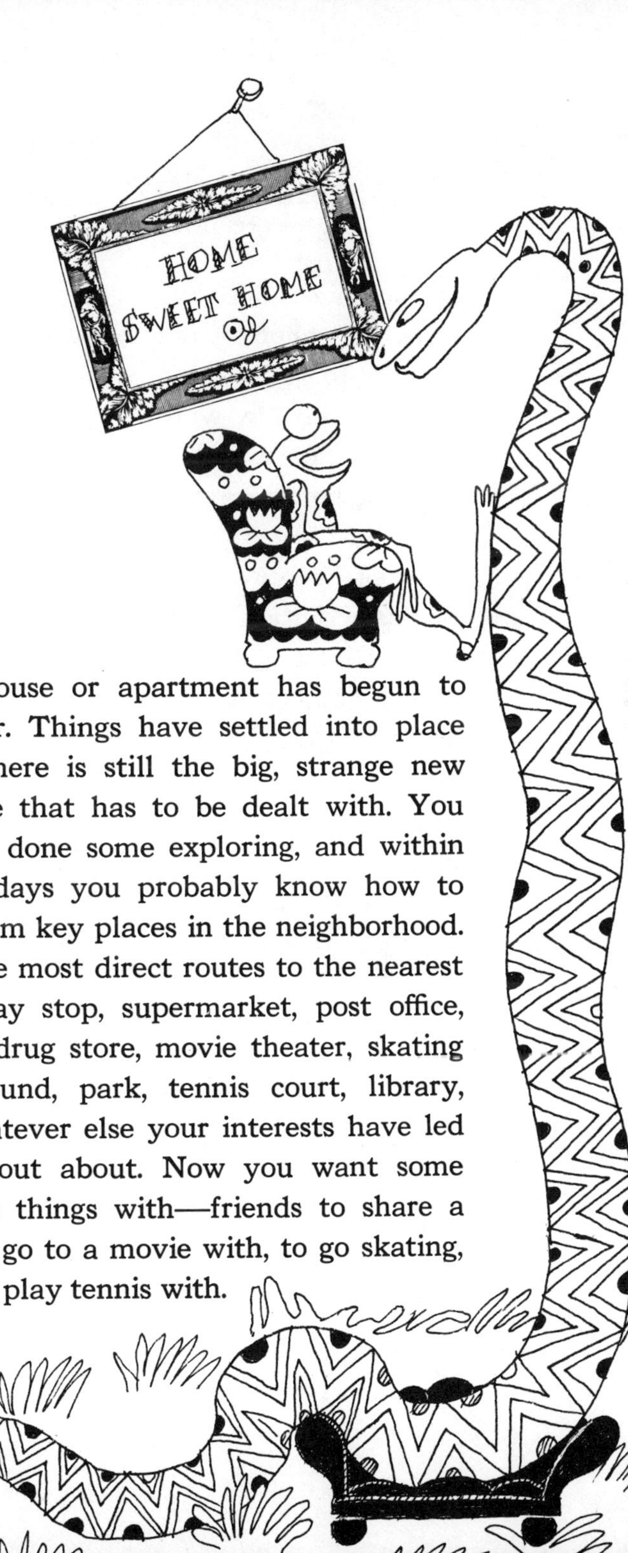

Your new house or apartment has begun to seem familiar. Things have settled into place inside, but there is still the big, strange new world outside that has to be dealt with. You have already done some exploring, and within a couple of days you probably know how to get to and from key places in the neighborhood. You know the most direct routes to the nearest bus or subway stop, supermarket, post office, candy store, drug store, movie theater, skating rink, playground, park, tennis court, library, "Y," and whatever else your interests have led you to find out about. Now you want some friends to do things with—friends to share a soda with, to go to a movie with, to go skating, swimming, or play tennis with.

IN THE GOOD OLD SUMMERTIME

If you have moved during the summer, you will have anywhere from several weeks to two months to get to know your new neighborhood and the people who live nearby before you have to start school. You will have time to feel at home before having to deal with a whole new group of teachers and classmates, and the pressures of homework, sports, and other extracurricular activities.

At first glance, your new neighborhood may seem bereft of boys and girls your own age, but that is not likely to be the case. Remember that summer is vacation time. (Your parents may have purposely scheduled the move at that time of the year so that they could use vacation days for packing and unpacking, and so that you would not have to change schools in the middle of a term.) A lot of the neighborhood kids may be away at camp or visiting relatives, but they won't all be away at the same time or for the whole summer. Those who are around may be a little lonely themselves and eager for someone to keep them company.

But you will not meet anyone by staying inside watching television. Don't let shyness turn you into a hermit. Get out of the house and start doing things that interest you. You are likely to find people who interest you doing the same things.

ACTIVITY INVENTORY

Here is just a short list of places and activities that can lead you to new acquaintances. (Add as many more as you can think of.)

The "Y"
Check out the summer schedule at the Y nearest you. Many "Ys" offer classes in swimming and tennis at reasonable prices. Learning and practicing a new skill with someone is a good way of getting to know that person. The "Y" also offers classes in all sorts of other areas ranging from needlecraft and guitar playing to modern dance and karate. Register for a class that appeals to you and you will probably meet some boys and girls you will want to know.

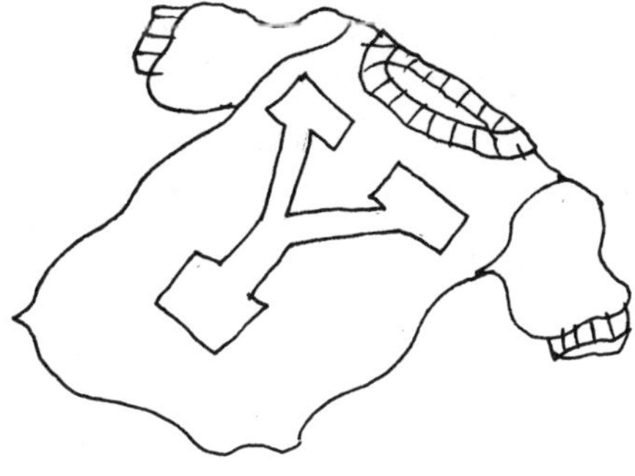

The community center

If there is a community center in your neighborhood it probably sponsors at least one activity that you enjoy: a ceramics workshop, a beginners' class in backgammon, or a woodworking course. This is another way of meeting boys and girls with interests similar to yours.

Running and jogging

Running and jogging have become such popular pastimes that there are tracks in almost every neighborhood. Find the one nearest you and you are sure to find some people who share your enthusiasm for the sport. You don't have to be an expert jogger, just a willing one. If you have never tried it before but think you would like it, now is a good time to start.

Skating

If you love to roller skate and there is a rink nearby, treat yourself to an afternoon of skating each week. By cutting down on soda and gum you can probably stretch your allowance to cover the cost. But you don't need a rink for skating if there is a smooth sidewalk in your neighborhood. Indoors or out, you are likely to come across others who enjoy skating as much as you do.

The same goes for skateboarding, of course.

Zoom down the street on your skateboard and you can be pretty sure that one of the kids in the neighborhood is going to join you—if only to try to impress you with his or her latest technique. A little rivalry can be the start of a long friendship.

Horseback riding

If you love horses, and your parents don't balk at the costs involved in riding (it is an expensive sport), sign up for a lesson at the local riding academy or stable. Getting to know the people who are learning with you will follow naturally.

BACK TO SCHOOL

If you moved in late August and did not have a chance to get to know any of your new schoolmates during the summer, you may be dreading those first few days of school. Anyone in that situation is bound to have a few panicky thoughts such as:

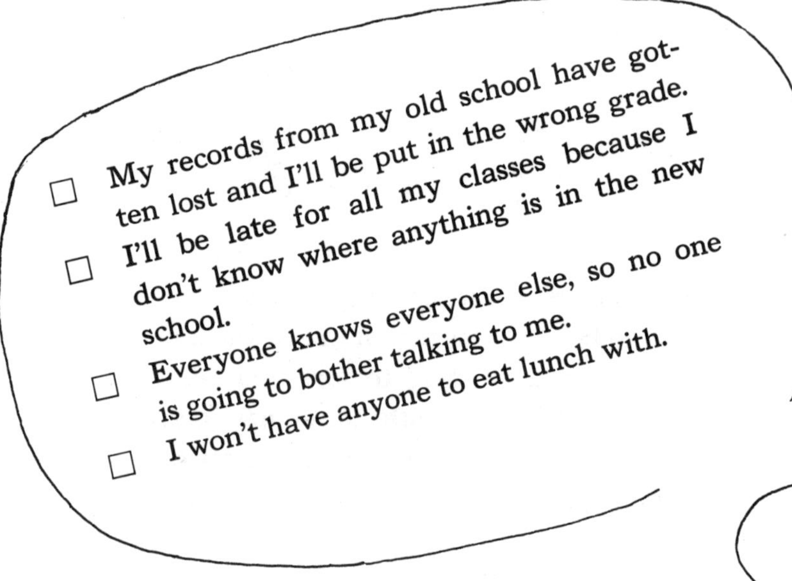

It is perfectly natural to have these thoughts, but try to remember that they are not entirely realistic and that there are things you can do to avoid some of the trouble spots.

As a new student, you will probably have to go to the school with your parents to register a few days before the term starts. At that point you will know that your records have been properly transferred and that you are enrolled at the right grade level. Since it may not occur to the grown-ups that you are worried about finding your way around the school building, let them know. Ask the registrar if you and your parents can look around the building to become familiar with it. Find out what entrance you are supposed to use; what time you are supposed to be in class; whether or not there are lockers for you to put your outer clothes and books in; what sort of lunchroom facilities there are; when the school day ends; and any other questions that are bothering you. The answers will not make all your anxieties disappear, but they will help you to feel more self-confident.

INTRODUCING THE NEW YOU

If you have had secret thoughts about changing your image, now is the time to give it a try. Instead of spending those days before school starts worrying about what is going to happen, give some thought to how you see yourself and how you want others to see you.

You go through a lot of physical and emotional changes as you grow from child to adolescent, so it is only natural that you have some new ideas about how you want to wear your hair, what sort of clothes appeal to you, and how you want to spend your school and leisure time. Let your new classmates meet the more mature you.

You may have been typecast at your old school as the athlete who wasn't interested in academic subjects, and as a result your fellow students didn't take you seriously when you talked about books or history. Your new classmates are not going to have that bias, so if you are informed and enthusiastic about almost any subject, those classmates who share your interests are likely to pay attention.

And just because you never used to care about how your hair or clothes looked does not mean you can't start caring now, and doing something about it. Your family may tease you at first when you suddenly start washing your hair every other day and blowing it dry, and you begin to exchange shapeless tee shirts and jeans for sleek shirts and pants. But your new acquaintances are simply going to accept you as someone who knows how to get it together.

Before you get caught up in the routine of school and start repeating old habits, think about new areas you would like to explore. Once you have decided what areas interest you most, find out what your new school has to offer in the way of courses and extracurricular activities to help you pursue those interests. Whatever you do out of your own enthusiasm is going to bring you into contact with boys and girls with whom you have things in common. Instead of sitting around feeling lonely and sorry for yourself during those last few days before school starts, spend the time getting to know the new you. Making another list might help. For example:

Interests Inventory

- ☐ Sports
- ☐ Languages
- ☐ Theater
- ☐ Drawing
- ☐ Music
- ☐ People

It is not hard to figure out how to apply your efforts in school to develop these interests. Try out for one or several of the school teams. Join the language club at school if there is one; if there isn't, think about getting together with a couple of other language students for an informal conversational session once or twice a week. You might combine your interest in theater and drawing by joining the after-school drama club and designing sets for new productions. Trying out for the school band or chorus will help you to meet people and make music at the same time. Having some specific ideas about what you want to do in school will make the new experience less scary.

THE FIRST DAY

You arrive at the right room, sit down at an unoccupied desk, and take a quick look around at your fellow students. They all seem to know one another and you feel left out—either totally ignored or under close scrutiny. You may be ignored—for the moment—while old friends exchange news about their vacations. You probably are being scrutinized—with interest—by boys and girls who are curious about the new person in class. You are curious yourself, so why shouldn't they be?

If you catch someone's eye, don't let your glance slide away or suddenly look down and start fumbling with your notebook. Smile at the person and he or she will probably smile back. Don't let your shyness make you look standoffish and unfriendly. Let the other person know you are approachable. And if your braces make you feel self-conscious about smiling, try to forget about it! Many of your new classmates will have similar hardware. Remember, a few years from now you will all have gorgeous even teeth to show for it.

Your classmates may feel a little shy about approaching you. Do your best to meet them halfway, and try not to make snap judgments. Before class starts, introduce yourself to the people sitting near you, and listen carefully when they tell you their names so that you can call them by name when you see them in the hall later that day or the next. You can't tell much about a person from a quick look and a hello; get to know something about a person before deciding whether or not he or she is someone you want for a friend.

Remember, too, that your arrival has added a new and possibly exciting element to your classmates' lives. Many of them are as eager to find out about you as you are to know about them. You don't have to barrage new acquaintances with questions, but do make it clear that you are interested in learning about them, and be fairly informative in your comments and replies. It is hard to keep an exchange going if you are answering simply yes or no, so polish up your conversational skills.

MOVING DURING THE MIDTERM

The problems of settling in at school and getting to know people in the middle of the term are not too different from those you face coming in at the beginning of the school year. But since the term has already begun, you may feel a bit bewildered about where to begin with homework, reports, special projects, etc.

One way to get a head start on dealing with that situation is to get a class study program from the new school before you arrive. That is easy to arrange if you have a preview of the school, but if you are not able to visit the school before moving, a written request will probably bring you the information you want. It is very helpful to know in advance what your teachers will expect of you. If you are up to date on schoolwork, you will be better able to concentrate on finding your way around the new place and making new friends.

If the new school is ahead of the old school academically, try to catch up as quickly as possible—before you even start at the new school if that can be managed. Don't be afraid to ask questions of your new teachers and classmates. They won't expect you to know everything immediately, and besides, most people like to be asked for information or advice.

Perhaps the new school is more advanced in math or science or foreign language studies. If you feel you need special help, be sure to let your new teacher know. He or she can work with you to plan a catch-up program and maybe suggest someone to coach you.

If you are lucky and your new class is just

learning something you had covered weeks ago at the old school, count your blessings, but don't be a show-off. If you are a little bored with going over things that you already know, ask the teacher to suggest some related, more advanced work you can do in the same subject area. If one of your new classmates is having trouble with the subject and is not too shy to ask you for help, that is a comfortable way to get to know that person.

When you move in the middle of the term, school activities are in full swing. You may feel left out for the first week or so because everyone already has a science project partner, the lunchtime cliques are formed, the gym class teams are complete, and all the roles in the class play have been assigned. Don't let it get you down though. Be friendly and as relaxed as possible. Participate in the ongoing activities without trying to displace someone else. You don't have to have an acting role to share in the excitement of putting on a play. There are almost never enough stagehands or behind-the-scenes assistants, so don't hesitate to volunteer for one of these less glamorous jobs if you are interested in getting into the school drama group. It's a good learning experience and an easy way of getting to know some of your new schoolmates.

It may be too late in the term to get on one of the school teams, but you can let the coach know you are interested in trying out next term. And in the meantime you can be practicing your basket shots and softball pitches, or improving your swimming speed.

By lunchtime of your first day at school you will probably know at least a few of your classmates by name. If one of them doesn't ask you to join them for lunch, the chances are it is just because they are a little shy or totally unaware of what it's like to be a newcomer. Get your own shyness under control and ask one of those new people to share your lunch table. Even if it's not so easy at first to make conversation, it is more fun than eating by yourself, and it is a good way to get to know your classmates.

Teams and cliques and groups are usually more flexible than they seem at first glance, and if you have interest and enthusiasm to offer, you will soon find yourself sharing the fun as well as the work.

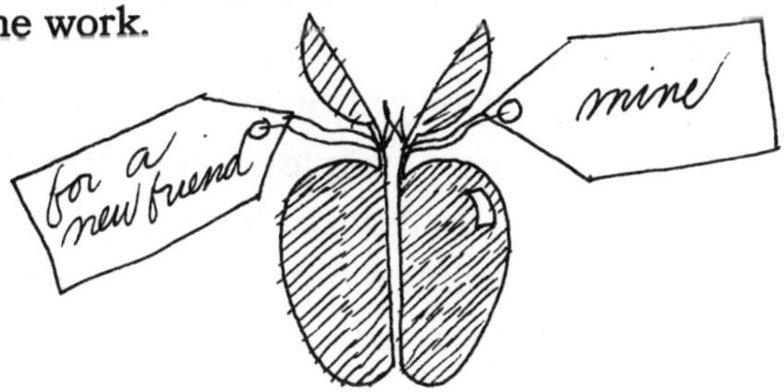

for a new friend

mine

DO YOU SPEAK THE SAME LANGUAGE?

If you have moved from one part of the country to another, you and your new acquaintances may have slightly different vocabularies. People move more often and over greater distances these days than they did a half century ago; and television links all parts of the country, so regional differences in lifestyles and language are disappearing. Nonetheless, you will probably find that your new friends use a few unfamiliar words.

Perhaps what you call a milk shake, they refer to as a frappe. You put on your jeans to go to school while your nextdoor neighbor wears dungarees. In the lunchroom, the girl sitting next to you asks if you want to share a sweet roll, which looks just like a Danish pastry to you. After basketball practice one of the guys on the team suggests stopping for a submarine and some pop, and pretty soon you are calling them that too, instead of a hero or hoagie and a soda.

Believe it or not, it will not be long before you and the new people around you are speaking the same language. You will not only be sharing a common vocabulary, but interests and experiences as well. Almost before you realize it, the new neighborhood will feel like home. The sea of unfamiliar faces at school will have sorted itself into favorite friends and teachers, casual acquaintances, rivals, and perhaps an ogre or two.

Moving does make you feel uprooted while you are in the midst of leaving the old and settling into the new. Remember that that feeling passes quickly, and that it is accompanied by the excitement and adventure of exploring the unknown. Think of this move, and any others you make in the future, as a chance to discover a new *you* as well as a host of new friends and experiences.

FOR FURTHER READING

Hobbies, Jobs, Activities

Moving time is a time of change and growth. And it's a good time to develop new interests and activities. Here are some books that will give you ideas and information about all sorts of hobbies and job possibilities.

Gilfond, Henry. *Genealogy: How to Find Your Roots.* New York: Franklin Watts, 1978.

Saunders, Rubie. *Baby Sitting.* New York: Franklin Watts, 1972.

Smaridge, Norah, and Hunter, Hilda. *The Teen-ager's Guide to Collecting Practically Anything.* New York: Dodd, Mead, 1972.

——— *The Teen-ager's Guide to Hobbies for Here and Now.* New York: Dodd, Mead, 1974.

Sweeney, Karen O'Connor. *How to Make Money.* New York: Franklin Watts, 1977.

Home, Fitness, Grooming

Moving to a new place means meeting new people. You want you and your home to look great. These books will give you tips for putting your best foot forward and having fun with new friends.

Alexander, Mary Jean. *Designing Your Own Room.* New York: Franklin Watts, 1977.

Benziger, Barbara. *Controlling Your Weight.* New York: Franklin Watts, 1973.

Lewis, Nancy, and Lewis, Richard. *Keeping in Shape.* New York: Franklin Watts, 1976.

Saunders, Rubie. *Good Grooming for Boys.* New York: Franklin Watts, 1972.

——— *Good Grooming for Girls.* New York: Franklin Watts, 1976.

——— *Quick and Easy Housekeeping.* New York: Franklin Watts, 1977.

Sweeney, Karen O'Connor. *Entertaining.* New York: Franklin Watts, 1978.

Self-Awareness

To be comfortable with other people you have to be comfortable with yourself. These books will help you to understand your own feelings better and to enjoy the adventure of making new friends.

Kalb, Jonah, and Viscott, David. *What Every Kid Should Know.* Boston: Houghton Mifflin, 1976.

Leicht, Katherine F. *Understanding Yourself.* New York: Franklin Watts, 1973.

Lipke, Jean C. *Dating.* Minneapolis: Lerner Publications, 1971.

Morrison, Carl, and Morrison, Dorothy V. *Can I Help How I Feel?* New York: Atheneum, 1976.

INDEX

ABOUT THE AUTHOR

Carolyn Trager has been active in several areas of the children's book world for most of her professional life. She holds a full-time position as a senior editor with a New York publishing house, where she works on both adult and juvenile titles. In addition, she finds time to write juvenile nonfiction and to teach a workshop on writing for children as well as another course about book publishing. Her current book, the first for Franklin Watts, is based on a wealth of practical experience: the author has moved no less than fourteen times! Ms. Trager lives and works in New York City.